SCIENCE AND THE CRISIS IN SOCIETY

Science and the Crisis in Society

FRANK H. GEORGE

Professor, Institute of Cybernetics, Brunel University,
Kingston Lane, Uxbridge, Middlesex

WILEY-INTERSCIENCE
a division of John Wiley & Sons Ltd.
London — New York — Sydney — Toronto

Library of Congress Catalog Card No. 73–138672

ISBN 0 471 29630 9

Printed in Great Britain by
Unwin Brothers Limited
Woking and London

FOR CAMBRIDGE
on July 12th, 1947

"I'll love you dear, I'll love you
till China and Africa meet . . ."
                    W. H. Auden

Preface

THERE IS INEVITABLY some delay in conceiving of, writing and publishing a book. In this case the delay has been minimal, but even so the first plans for its writing were laid down in 1968 and the writing and re-writing took quite a long time. Thanks to the publishers, the time taken to convert the typescript into a book has been miraculously quick, but even so I have carefully watched for any signs of a departure from my predictions. By and large the main events that have occurred have simply confirmed what the text predicts, but in watching the world evolve I have been aware of many facets which might have been mentioned and were not, and these are being reserved for a future book. Such facets, in any case, are largely more private and personal than can be discussed in terms of the application of science.

It still seems to me to be the case that we are heading for some of the most momentous decisions that have ever faced humanity, and they are all concerned with the explosion of knowledge. Communication and control, especially in the field of Cybernetics, are progressing in a way that makes society increasingly out-of-joint with the times. The problems of government and the world economic pressures continue to build up. Racial problems continue on a knife-edge, but there are some signs that the problems are at least being recognized.

The same applies to threats to individual liberty, especially by computer control, and there is a gradual awakening to the dangers of totalitarianism. It is quite clear now that there is a threat to the family, even if there is only as yet a mild awareness of the threat of a super-species.

All in all there are grounds for optimism, and the fact that social evolution is now seen to be accelerating fast, is making us all question all our old standards and values. This is a necessary, if often painful, part of human development.

FRANK GEORGE
Beaconsfield 1970

Contents

1 Basic Issues

"The sun shines down on the ships at sea,
It shines on you and it shines on me
Whatever we are or are going to be."

Poem XVIII, from "Look Stranger"
W. H. Auden

". . . Since the Army discovered that imagination is a major factor
in producing cowardice they have trained the Maskelyne breed in
the virtues of counter-imagination; a sort of amnesia . . ."

"Mountolive"
Lawrence Durrell

THIS IS A PERIOD of worldwide social unrest; it is a period
when colour problems, war, political quarrelling and the like
have never before been so prominent in world affairs. It is also
a time when old ideas and standards are changing at a rate which
leaves too many of us without a clear vision of what we either
can or should be doing.

This is also a period when science has become all-pervading
and influences us in ways of which we never dreamed in the
past. Today, more aspects of life are influenced by science than
ever before in the whole history of human civilization.

We must remember that science is concerned with predicting events, understanding events, and as a result of that
predicting and understanding, controlling events. It has also
played a vitally important part in developing the ability to
communicate, and it is no coincidence that the social unrest in
the world and science have developed hand in hand.

The first and most obvious point to make is that communication has made it possible for young people in particular, and all

sections of the communities of the world in general, to make their views known all over the world in a way which has never been possible before. The effect has been that of highlighting social problems, and a demand for solutions which has never reached anything like this peak in the whole history of civilization. This is indeed no coincidence, but the inevitable result of scientific development and social change. We shall argue that we are now going through an inevitable part of social evolution; we are now beginning to realize effectively the implications of the society in which we were brought up and we shall see, especially in Britain, the emphasis on greater social equality. We shall also see a further reaction against the Victorian era which both brought the last generation into being and supplied its values.

We are now being asked questions which we have never been asked before. We now need to have answers which we have never needed before. All this comes about because for the first time in the whole history of human society we are being asked what are our aims and goals in living, what are the consequences of our actions and what are the logical consequences of our decisions in the form of rules, laws and moral precepts. So it is we have to be systematic and make predictions in a way which in the past was never thought even remotely possible or indeed desirable.

Characteristic of this change is the attitude of the university student towards authority: he no longer regards authority as something which is inevitably right and to be diligently followed. Much the same is seen in the attitude of a person towards his job; he no longer feels that his employer is necessarily right. Perhaps it was never the case that they thought their superiors or their employers were right, but for the first time there has been some machinery whereby comments, criticisms and questions can be made rather than decisions automatically accepted when provided *ex cathedra*.

At the same time as these inevitable social changes are going on, we are confronted with a great deal of violence and hatred and the development of what seem like new vices. Certainly the widespread use of drugs and the fast development of a very much more permissive society suggest that we ought at least to consider whether our own moral standards of the past have any value today. What are we to do about it? Are we to change our ideas, or are we to go on thinking of our moral views as something invariant under all circumstances and perhaps given by external decree?

Certainly there is a need for new crosses to bear, because the very decay of religious influence is a major factor in determining our present social course. It seems that ideas on morals must change, and merely to say that they are invariant and inviolable is simply to exacerbate the social unrest that is already going on and, as a result, give an unfortunate direction to that unrest. The sort of unfortunate direction that can be given by non-acceptance (or outright opposition), for example, is to drive something underground. Driving problems underground, and here one thinks of prostitution as an example, is not to eliminate them, but merely to ensure that they get out of the public eye; they are swept under the carpet, and become even less controllable. This is precisely the process we must avoid; we must make our social problems explicit, face them, and not assume that because nothing wrong is ever heard nothing wrong ever occurs.

Another feature of the decay of religious influence that we must face is the fact that we cannot assume any longer that we are "God's chosen people". We cannot any longer assume that we are bound to survive under all circumstances, and that goodness and right will eventually win the battle of survival. None of these things is any longer acceptable. We ourselves, by the nature of our control over our lives, which is all the time increasing, mostly to our own embarrassment, can direct our future. This is the only basis by which we can ensure survival of the species, if that is what is desired.

It is explicit recognition that it is our own need to control ourselves rather than appeal to some outside source of power that has caused some large part of our predicament. It is natural that people who have lived satisfactorily, at least in their own eyes, in the past should say, "Why change the existing state of affairs; that control is still the best and we should stick with it". Whether this is true or not, and whether religion is factual or fictional, is not now relevant. What is relevant is that people today no longer accept statements *ex cathedra*.

If we do not accept the facts of social change, the alternative could be death or extinction, or even worse; it might take the form of slavery. We must accept that change is the key and science is the means of using the key to unlock the door to the future. We are, by virtue of education and genetics, rather inadequate in our ability to make quick changes. Everything about society and its present structure, everything about human beings and their present psychology, suggests that change shou ld be slow; the trouble is that in fact it is fast—and if it turned out to be too fast for us, we ourselves would become victims of natural selection.

One of the biggest problems that we have to face is the problem of *complexity*. Most of us are in extremely complicated social situations. We are often at the centre of webs of activity operating at many levels, most of which we have never explicitly faced in the past. Rather than try to sort out the complexities of the situation and find some sort of solutions, we fall back on what we have always depended upon, the easy axioms which allow us to be guided in our general behaviour. Complexity can be seen easily in social situations involving one's own parents and one's own children. The relationship of people, one to the other, is an exceptionally complicated and difficult matter and the subject of so much modern artistic activity in the form of plays and novels. This is a field where science has yet to catch up effectively with the complexities of the problem.

There is no adequate science of social relationships in existence, and yet to fail to understand the complexities of human relationships is to fail to understand the intensely complicated nature of society. Every time we pass a new law or every time in the family we pass a new edict we are unaware, more often than not, of the implications and the effect upon the society for which the edict is passed.

It is this we have to work out in detail; it is this that science can do for us. It is this that science is doing, and in some ways making it very much more difficult for people to organize the world in which we all live. Part of the reason for this new difficulty, of course, is the decaying of the old way of life which lingers on, often in places of power, trying to preserve the methods of the past and hoping very much not to be concerned, partly from a feeling of inadequacy at the particular game, with the methods of the future.

Against this background of quickly changing standards, and with the arrival of a human science, not often recognized by most conventional scientists themselves, a certain amount of confusion is bound to reign. Add to this the fact that there is no complete substitute for human experience, add to this that as a result of the swing against Victorianism and as a development of the permissive society it has been increasingly difficult to induce notions of self-discipline, and some shadowy outline of our problem begins to emerge.

The great virtue of conventional Christianity was the insistence on self-discipline. This has largely gone and one of our biggest single problems will be to try to find some substitute. There is also the complication of motivation, the need for long-term and short-term goals. What are people to do with their lives? In the past, under fear of unemployment and poverty, most people clung to the very business of survival, but inevitably, as conditions become better and better, more and more people—still by no means enough—have more time and more independence, more freedom to consider what life is really about. They cannot easily fall back on the injunctions of a George Bernard Shaw, who suggested one should go on living, and living busily, and not ask why one was living. We are now asking why we are living, we are now asking what is the purpose of life, and there are many different possible answers to this, some of which are not by any means acceptable.

Science is only a means, many people tell us, but the principal means for all that, whereby certain ends are achieved; but what are these ends? The ultimate end could be complete boredom and futility. It can also be argued that the means are really the ends, as is so often the case in ordinary physical activities in life. Everything seems to be in the means and the end merely a consummation. It is possible that there is some broader purpose in life than merely to survive in comfort, and this is where religion again comes in, but on the whole the feeling at the moment is against this view; most people think of the world as a scientific accident and something which, if it is to have a meaning, must have meaning which is imposed upon it by us ourselves. So perhaps the best, or the most likely, of all views to take at the moment is that there are a series of purposes which we can impose on our own lives to ameliorate the society in which we live and we should avoid, utterly eschew indeed, talk of ultimate goals.

As immediate purposes we can easily see that we ought to better the physical condition of man, try to cope with sickness and disease as well as poverty, and more positively avoid slavery and the enslavement of people in social systems which are dedicated to ends, good or bad, but if they involve slavery cannot in any sense be good for the people as a whole. We must somehow exploit and develop the positive features of the universe so that physical life becomes increasingly bearable. But all the time one is aware that this is only a relative thing that somehow seems inadequate as an end in itself.

We shall, in this opening chapter, provide a few guesses as to what it is we are supposed to do with our lives and how it is that we can best do it. The book itself is intended to try to analyse these things in much greater detail, with its emphasis on science and education, and at the end we shall consider whether the initial guesses were right or not and, in so far as they are right, whether they have been justified by our analysis and examination of a large number of facts.

We shall assume now that in the short term safe, peaceful survival of the world community of human beings is an essential goal. We shall also assume that we must do everything we can to make sure that no human being is discriminated against on account of his colour, his race or his creed. These seem to be basic principles which, although people pay them lip service, very few agree to in practice. Therefore perhaps most important of all is the real belief that these things are worthwhile goals, not that they are goals that everyone should pay lip service to and no more. This is not necessarily to exclude the possibility of individuals gaining power, some individual countries being more powerful than others, it is not to say that egalitarianism should be worldwide, since it seems a fact about human individuals, even human races, that they are not all equal by the very nature of things; they should though at least have the opportunity to realize their potential to the full. If in the course of time it turns out that they are all more or less equal, so be it; that will automatically reveal itself if they are given the necessary opportunity.

The means by which these goals might be achieved, if acceptable as short-term aims, are clearly through:

(1) education: this is bound to be a key point in any development of a world social system.

(2) flexibility of outlook and the ability to change one's subgoals or short-term goals as circumstances change. This is absolutely essential.

(3) the acceptance of the notion of change. This is an absolutely basic need. The realization that there are certain precepts, rules or codes that we hold today that we need not necessarily hold tomorrow; it is seemingly a scientific fact that everything is quicksand and nothing is bedrock. We are not suggesting that this is necessarily the case, but the attitude which accepts this as an approximation to the case seems to be a better basis for the acceptance of social evolution than any other.

(4) the setting up of social standards which would replace in more objective ways the standards which have been given us *ex cathedra* by various religions in the past.

(5) a close consideration of religion and its relation to human motivation. Can we bring it up to date? Can we rejuvenate it? Do we have to abandon it, or can we find a substitute? If it is assumed a substitute is absolutely necessary, what form must the substitute take?

(6) selective control of our world. It is no longer sensible as an answer to world problems to say that everything must be controlled. Overcontrol of systems is just as deathly to human survival as undercontrol. What we most need to do is use our science to find out how much control is needed and where it should be exercised, and then leave systems absolutely alone where control is thought thoroughly undesirable. It is neither planning nor absence of planning that are virtues in themselves; what is important is to realize where each is appropriate.

(7) the initiation of self-discipline by other means than through enslavement, whether harsh scholastic discipline or religious discipline.

No doubt these short-term goals are by themselves inadequate, but we shall say virtually nothing about long-term goals except for the need for the survival of the community and its gradual betterment.

Let us now return to science and scientific methods for the moment, since this remains the main tool by which all these aims are to be achieved. Science is concerned very much with control. At the moment we control many aspects of society and many aspects of our environment. Soon we shall control the weather around us and other aspects of our society, all the time extending the ability to organize and carry out activities in the best interest of the people carrying out those activities. It leaves us with a question as to whether this should be the primary end of the society in which we live. What worries us, or should worry us, is that there are implications over and above those which are intended. It seems to place society more on a "knife-edge" than ever and the balance of power of different social aspects seems to be more critical than ever before. In short, our increasing ability, primarily through science, to control our own evolution creates more problems than it solves and yet is something from which we cannot retreat.

Consider the problem of controlling the weather. When the time comes when we can control our weather for the short term and our climate for the long term we shall have created enormous problems to solve as to what sort of weather is desirable and for whom. Rather in the same way as we organize our air services at the moment, or our train services, we tend to talk about what is best for the majority, or least costly to the community, or most profitable to the company; the same argument is always applied also to morality. Now in the type of economic climate in which we live, demand and its relation to supply dominates our thinking, and the idea of the good of the majority dominates our moral thinking, at least in theory. We must ask ourselves very carefully in the future whether these are the considerations which should be paramount. Perhaps inevitably such considerations lead among other things to a world, a "one world" made up of one single nation, but is this then to mean that each and every aspect of the nation should fail to be competitive; it could be that the whole plan of an organized world for the betterment of the majority would destroy the very basis on which it was built.

We shall be talking in some detail about science, especially scientific method, since this is clearly the major feature of our whole outlook, and we shall be saying more than once that science is concerned with prediction, with understanding and ultimately control. One tries to understand things mainly so that one can control them, and even if one does not always want to control things in detail but provide a general framework in which control could take place, one may still expect that there will always be other people who will be motivated to exercise the fullest control wherever this is possible. This immediately implies the enormous danger of scientific development and the possibility of control being exercised by people who may not be exercising it in the interests of the community as a whole. Or, to put it another way, since the interests of the community as a whole is not necessarily the right concept, then one can say that such control exercised by the wrong people can be vastly injurious to the development of the human race. Once more we feel that we are treading on quicksand all the time and virtually nothing is bedrock. That is the lot of the human being, and to appreciate this is to appreciate the nature of the problems with which we are confronted.

Somewhere in this total context of the complexity of individual and social relationships, the purposes and goals of people, the means to achieve these goals through material and non-material methods, somewhere among this kaleidescope are things which will change dramatically and we have to try to be aware of them when they occur.

Just two instances will be given of this point, although we shall return to it later. It may be that our concept of time is completely wrong, and we should not think in terms of ordered activities as future and past, etc. There are many communities in the world, such as the Hopi Indians, who do not think in terms of time as a flowing thing, like a river, which starts and finishes. If we, for example, lived many times longer than we do, tending more towards immortality, then the emphasis would be taken away from temporal change, which is partly measured by the span of our own life. With the development of science such a possibility becomes an obvious one and could completely change our attitude towards the society in which we live.

The second example is the so-called body–mind problem. The idea that bodies have minds, which has given way gradually during the twentieth century to the assumption that bodies are an integral thing and a mind is merely the performance of some aspects of a body, could eventually give way to the idea that mind was completely independent of body and did not require the body's services. We shall not attempt to pursue the consequences of this thought here, nor try to decide what possible justification there is for holding it; all that we are now concerned with saying is that should two such dramatic changes occur then the whole fabric in which we are thinking at one time can be completely changed for another time. Here lies our problem. Again, all is quicksand and nothing is bedrock. So, as usual, we must learn to "play the probabilities" and try to decide, in terms we can rely on as at least relatively reliable, what steps we should take into the future of society; we must establish short-term goals and try to recognize their consequences.

We must from the start take the view that there is always hope for survival, we should not be despondent, we must find a method to deal with the complexity of the problems with which we shall be confronted. We are going to succeed; we must succeed. But precisely because we are so determined, precisely because we are optimistic, we must be absolutely faithful to the process of discovering what the facts are, we must never skate around the possibilities of a particular development; let us always look carefully at the realities of the situation, and face their likely consequences.

We shall be saying many times that because of our very ability to produce artificially intelligent control systems—such as we see in automation—we might ourselves well produce a species that supersedes us. If this is the case, let us face it, because only by facing it can we be given anything like a chance to ensure that the very thing we most fear, and yet supply ourselves, can be stopped from happening.

Now let us turn in the next chapter to the business of forecasting; this is essentially a scientific business.

2 Past, Present and Future

"I care not if you bridge the seas,
 Or ride secure the cruel sky,
 Or build consummate palaces
 Of metal or of masonry.
 But have you wine and music still,
 And statues and a bright-eyed love,
 And foolish thoughts of good and ill
 And prayers to them who sit above?"

"To a Poet a Thousand Years Hence"
James Elroy Flecker

THE PROBLEM of forecasting accurately is not just that of guessing what will happen, but rather saying what will happen *if* we do certain things and do not do others. This, of course, implies speculating as to what we probably will do, and at the same time trying to determine what we *should* do. We shall also be thinking in terms of such principles as "maximizing our options" and trying to decide when an action is reversible and when it is not. We prevent children leaping off a cliff primarily because the experiment is usually irreversible.

It is a basic principle that people should make decisions whenever possible in the light of their *overall* objectives. So we ought to be constantly asking ourselves what sort of society we want to emerge on the surface of this earth, or even on the stars and planets of this galaxy. Only then can we make intelligent statements about current trends and policies in all the various aspects of our lives. Only by such means can we say what *should* be done both now and in the future.

Robert Jungt has made the point that there exists no "science of the future"; it sems incredible, but there is no research being undertaken into the future of society. No chair nor institute has yet been set up to deal systematically with trends and developments which directly affect the whole of our lives and our progress as human beings.

Although science itself predicts, it is generally used to predict rather specific, and relatively short-term, purposes. We are now talking of longer-term forecasting with respect to general as well as specific issues. The problem is that of goals. If we do not know the next goals we should be aiming at, we cannot sensibly decide upon the immediate and necessary policies to achieve those goals.

Erich Jantsch has also made a relevant point that we shall quote:

> "For centuries the future has been largely determined by haphazard technical developments. Today technological forecasting is being used to outline the scope of technical innovation and to influence its direction and pace. In this way man is becoming the master of his technology, where previously he was its slave."

The development of manned lunar colonies, the developments in the field of new sources of energy from fossils, the sea or even the rotation of the earth, could absolutely change the nature of human life. In planning for the future, we must take account of as many of these possibilities as we can and try to estimate if and when their emergence is likely.

This is the next phase of our development, and in carrying it through we must remember what we have already said about the second phase danger, which would in turn make us slaves again and not master.

In talking of the future we could easily let our imagination run riot, for it is this that makes humans different from animals—their almost unlimited imaginative gift. We could easily imagine, for example, a situation where today was Jupiter Day! The rockets are paying a special trip from all earth rocket bases and from all other planetary bases to Jupiter, to celebrate its colonization. Unlikely? No, surely not; almost certain, the only question is, *when?*

The date is AD 2000. Twenty years ago they first landed on Jupiter—the trip was made from the moon—and last year we saw the first settlement set up and the first city built there.

Such a picture may seem in 1970 to be a false one, but the spirit of the picture is quite right. We shall colonize space in the same way as our forefathers colonized the surface of the earth. This is not, though, by any means the only important step that will be taken by the year 2000. Cancer will almost certainly be as universally curable by then as tuberculosis is now, and this for many people would be regarded as a far more important development than that of colonization.

We shall expect to fly around the earth at supersonic speeds, and we expect highspeed monorails to operate between our cities. The cities themselves may be vast linear organizations spreading from Aberdeen to Naples, or Boston to New Orleans, and the distribution and composition of the population will have changed from its present form beyond all recognition. Needless to say, we may also expect carefully planned parking spaces and highspeed transfer systems within, as well as between, our cities. That is until the need for physical travel declines and people communicate in much more detailed form from their own homes.

The development of communication systems with the main emphasis on interstellar flight is too obvious to make much of— this is a typical child of science. Forecasts for the future exploration of space on an interplanetary basis are likely to occur in the 70s, as is permanent occupation of the moon. The more general implications for science, and its ability to investigate space, to say nothing of its social implications for human beings, are almost without limit.

More fundamental in some ways, though, is the emergence of internationalism—a unity—on the surface of the earth. We may expect also the disappearance of the family unit, the disappearance of colour differences, but not of prejudice. Prejudice is one stage more basic psychologically than the particular issues over which prejudice operates at any given time.

We may be, above all, on the brink of substitution of appearance for reality, and this is the reason we may no longer need to travel, at least not as frequently. After all, do we really want to go from Vienna to Melbourne? The sense in which we want to go can be sufficiently provided for by science. The letter and the telephone are only the first steps towards the full sensory message which can be sent without involving actual physical travel, except on the part of electromagnetic waves.

This last point brings us near to another set of themes we want to deal with: the themes of human adaptation, imagination and suggestibility and the question as to how, as science develops, these vital human features will also develop, how they will change and in turn change society itself.

We have other themes too, if we may drive home the point by repetition. The advance of science automatically means the increase of the *control* we have on our environment. On the other hand, increased communication which is vital to control serves the ends of better education and better understanding. Here again we have something of a paradox, since this very control element could lead to a degree of what we shall call totalitarian control—and that degree *could* far exceed anything we have so far understood by the name "fascism". Communication on the other hand, while still serving control, also serves what is in some sense the opposite, freedom through education and understanding.

Another of our themes is that of hedonism. We want to be happy and we mean to be, and we wish to avoid pain, and the question is how, for us as an adapting species, we should best succeed. All the time boredom is at the back of our minds as our worst enemy, the enemy of happiness.

Cybernetics, which is one of our newest sciences, is called the science of control and communication, and control and communication is also what most of life is concerned with. The future of communication has been written about extensively and we shall not neglect to discuss it, but control is our major theme. This, of course, has been written about too. George Orwell has given us a picture of a possible date for 1984 where the whole emphasis was on thought control; the behaviouristic view was also made clear in Aldous Huxley's *Brave New World*. In *Ape and Essence* Huxley had used sex as a driving force to keep the community motivated; again the emphasis is on control. Modern business, as of 1970, thinks of money as the primary motivator, but with the advent of automation and increased leisure this may change; the question is how and for what?

The older Utopia builders, including Sir Thomas More himself, and Samuel Butler with his dream state *Erewhon*, were concerned with social organization from a more political viewpoint, and less from a scientific point of view.

There are one or two comments which must be made here. First, even in the short term, which is what we are discussing, we are *not* trying to build Utopia, unless Utopia is the name for the next phase of the ever-changing evolutionary picture. The greatest feature of man is his imagination and adaptability. Provide him with a *fixed* Utopia and immediately and automatically when achieved it ceases to be Utopia. We have somehow to provide an ever-changing stream of experience, and as our control over nature increases we have no means of being sure that this will automatically be supplied for us.

The criticism of Huxley's *Brave New World*, and one we must bear in mind all the time, is that the storyteller, who hated every minute of what he saw in the new world, had himself not *evolved* in it. Everyone hates and fears the unfamiliar, and a sudden large step in evolution would inevitably cause revolution or mass psychosis. In other words, whatever happens people can get to, or even be made to, accept it—or this is nearly always so, at least up to now. This power of adaptation becomes more and more possible as our power of control continues to improve, but the demand is also greatly increased and so the struggle continues.

Fascism in its most extreme forms must be much more successful in the future than it has been in the past. But will it, on account of human adaptability, bring about its own destruction? If so, what will replace it? History at best only answers this for isolated countries such as Germany under Nazism; our question is about the whole of civilization.

We are going to try to understand, through looking carefully at science and the humanities, what trends are likely to be capable of development to the point of usefulness in the next thirty years. On this will depend the sort of world we *can* have, in the short term. We should provide ourselves with many clearcut issues which are worth working for. We shall also, though, make a serious attempt to predict what actually will happen.

Man is our yardstick. We cannot spell out our overall goal; but the maximum good to the majority at the minimum expense to the minority is something like the necessary recipe, in the short term. But we must also, of course, try to understand what "good" is for different people at different times. It is clearly a relative thing in some sense, since what is good for you now depends so much on your actual circumstances, and these are changing all the time.

To be able to achieve even an approximation to our goal, we have to be able to perform some mental gymnastics. We need to be experts in computers and automation, in ethics and politics, in economics and sociology, in the arts, in religion, and also perhaps even in neurophysiology and psychology. The list is absurdly long and no one person can achieve expertise in so many different fields; we shall simply try to see the broad brush strokes of change in our society, and to do so we have to be able to take up many different points of view and see how these interact.

Here we have another problem. It is difficult for people to take up many different points of view and believe in them all sufficiently at the same time. Some less fortunate people find themselves unable to change at all from a single point of view, and while this is individually sad, for a whole community it becomes nothing less than a tragedy. It fixes and fossilizes the society, eventually destroys its capacity to evolve and thus destroys it; it is a partial failure of human adaptation.

"The problem of various viewpoints" can be easily illustrated. To a scientist in the full flush of enthusiasm for finding new facts, discovering principles or illuminating existing knowledge, the barrenness of the arts, of the words of poets, and the patterns of painters, can be an irritating distraction. To the man of letters, stimulated to excited visions by the tragedy of Hamlet, or the moving drama of a novel or a poem, the world of the scientist may seem parochial and dull.

That people exist who take and really feel the above two views is obvious enough, even if they do not often say so publicly, but rather pay lip service to the other person's point of view.

However, it also sometimes happens that these two views can appear alternatively in the *same* person. There is much benefit to be gained by such fluctuations since they allow of the development of a balanced, flexible outlook with a great breadth of vision.

The same thing happens even *within* a discipline; you can find yourself supporting different points of view at different times and find it difficult in one frame of mind to recapture the excitement and magic, or even the plausibility, of the other.

This processing or conditioning of men and women makes for lopsided attitudes to the world, and this is something which can stop us understanding how the various parts of the complex jigsaw puzzle fit together. It is on such a basis that prejudice and partiality feed.

Our real problem remains that man has developed and is developing at a faster and faster rate all the time, and the danger is that he will destroy himself by the power of his consciousness and abstract imaginative ability before he can be persuaded to look again at certain things, especially at life *and* death, from another, indeed from a whole series of new points of view.

Where are we going? Does the further future lie in science? In art? In religion? We have to give an answer to such questions and the method used may be rational, or scientific, but the facts discovered may be irrational; truth, for example, could be totally unpalatable. This is another important theme, and we must look at our problem now from various points of view, back and forth in time and space, and on different levels and from our various interconnected vantage points.

Another difficulty for man is the difficulty of dimensions. It is a familiar problem; we cannot readily have a feel for the unfamiliar. If you were told that the state of California spent $100,000,000 per annum on education (the figures are entirely mythical) you really would find it difficult, especially if you lived in England and knew little about California, to say whether this was enough or not. If your source of information got the figure wrong and said "$10,000,000" or "$1,000,000,000", most of us would probably not know the difference.

When we are told that it is 483,000,000 miles to Jupiter from the sun, we are loathe to comment since it could be twice as far or half as far and we simply would not know the difference without looking it up in a book. Then we remember that at the speed of a Concorde jet it would still take fifty years to travel this distance, and the mind boggles at the whole thought of interstellar flight.

Another example is that of speeds, especially the speeds of computers. An electronic computer can add and subtract in times which range from one-thousandth to one-millionth (or even less) of a second. This is from a thousand to a million times better than can be done by an ordinary electrical calculating machine, which is still far faster than it can be done by any man or woman.

Looked at in more familiar terms, there was a project on the waterways of the St. Lawrence River in Canada. It was estimated that the problems involved would take every available mathematician in Canada at least one hundred years to solve, yet these problems actually involved less than a week's computing time. Today the computing time would only be a matter of hours, and this change from weeks to hours has taken place in less than fifteen years.

The same problem applies to time as well as to everyday figures or astronomical distances. It is not easy to appreciate that human life has existed on this planet for about two million years. Such a thought makes the Greeks' vintage era—a mere six thousand years ago—seem like yesterday. Life itself emerged from the non-living—a difference only of degree, however important the difference—about two hundred million years ago. Only people like geologists, archaeologists and astronomers have a head for such dimensions, and only then in a limited way as a result of direct and regular contact with such vast—one is tempted to say astronomical—quantities. The sense of time is one of those features which seem most likely now to be destroyed as we can move backwards or forwards at will—at least such a backward and forward movement is what will soon be literally possible. It may be at the same time we shall no longer wish to emphasize the difference between reality and appearance.

There are still great difficulties in correctly picturing the universe in which we live. These difficulties are in some cases fairly obvious ones. In other cases they are not. One of the obvious ones is that we cannot, as it were, get outside the world and look in on it. Nor indeed is it easy to see what this would mean. Most of us have trouble with Einstein's edict that "the Universe is finite but unbounded", and some of the modern cosmological theories of the creation of the universe, whether continuous or otherwise, provide special difficulties for our imagination.

The inability to get outside our own experience and the need to explain all events in terms of that experience must leave us agnostic about the nature of the wider reality. It could all be the same as what we directly experience. It may even be that what we experience indirectly when helped by the equipment of modern science in the form of highpowered telescopes, microscopes and cyclotrons is representative, or what a statistician would call a typical sample of the whole of the universe. But there is *no way* in which we can be sure of this. This leads to the need to explain things often in anthropomorphic terms, where man and his immediate experience are the only yardstick.

There can be no doubt about such anthropomorphic explanations having played a large part in the past. Sir James Frazer, the eminent anthropologist, illustrates the point with one of many examples. In talking of the burial of an African chieftain he says:

> "The social position which he had on earth must be fully maintained in the life hereafter. To ensure his goodwill it is necessary to make periodic offerings at his grave. If these are neglected he will remind his relatives by appearing to them in dreams . . ."

Our forefathers were strongly inclined to the purely anthropomorphic. Here, although we rely on evidence from historians of ancient history and from anthropologists who studied so-called primitive tribes, we recognize intuitively from our own experience the temptation to explain events in purely personal terms. For our forefathers, when a man is swallowed by a crocodile in the nearby river it is an occurrence which is explained by the wrath of the spirit of his departed uncle. Similarly, for us, if something exists, it must have been created, created by someone or created by something?

But is it necessary to conceive of things as being created at all? Why should they not exist from time immemorial and for time everlasting? This is where we begin to have doubts about such notions as time. Having doubts that may not be easy to resolve or which are even incapable of being resolved at all is still perhaps better than having no doubt at all, although the other side of this coin is to admit that it may be better to have faith in something, or someone, rather than have no faith at all.

Everything is being referred back, and necessarily so, to our own experience. It would be self-contradictory, we argue, to deny the methods of logic; we only have to worry about its domain of application: is there anything beyond logic? If so, what does that mean? Since we cannot see beyond where we cannot see, and this is logically undeniable, we can, even must— if we are to discuss such further regions—speculate. If we speculate we may or may not be correct; we cannot tell. This could become rather like an argument over a matter of opinion as if it were a matter of fact.

Occam's razor, a famous logical device from the past, states in effect that of two equally plausible explanations we should accept the *simpler*. This is not always easy as a principle to apply, since we do not always agree as to which explanation is, in fact, the simpler. The group of early twentieth-century philosophers called the logical positivists tell us we should accept as true only what is capable of being verified. We could say "Why?" to both views and yet know that there are reasons for holding them. This is a case where stating evidence is not easy; there is a sort of pragmatic, or practical, ring about our approach. We accept methods if they seem to work.

But there is another side to all this. We talk of science, philosophy and logic as if it were the only manner of understanding the world. What about the artist's "truth of the heart"? Suppose we deny altogether the scientist and the logician, since they are unfamiliar to most people. Suppose, for example, we assert that what matters is people—the human predicament— and we may even talk of *spirit* here and provide a familiar speculative account of the human plight. We think now of love, affection, brotherhood, of life and of death; this is a very different sort of yardstick. Because of "the problem of various viewpoints" we are now led to a cleavage. We are going to argue that both points of view could be either right or wrong, but are not in any case mutually exclusive.

What we are saying now could be about religion and atheism, or agnosticism or whatever term is preferred for someone who disbelieves, for example, the claims of Christianity about the nature of reality.

Suppose at this point you argue that problems which we try to solve and explanations which we try to give are always *with some goal in mind*. If a man says to me "What is electricity?" I hesitate because I can answer the question in a variety of ways. I might say "It is the source of our lights", and I would demonstrate how throwing a switch lights a bulb and throwing it again turns it out. This is what a child or a very simple person might expect by way of answer. I might say, though, "It is like water flowing in a pipe, and if you throw a switch you dam up the pipe". I may refer to electron theory, or finally I might say "I don't know", since the person who is asking me the question now turns out to be a quantum physicist. Similarly, a problem is often solved "to some extent", rather than absolutely. We build a bridge which is sufficiently strong to withstand certain strains.

If we now apply such a view to the problems of humanity, we may say that much depends on what our goal is. We are suggesting that we live in a world devoid of absolutes. But we must be careful here, since to assert this would seem like asserting something absolute. Then we should fall foul of logic, indeed of our own logic, since we should have said something self-contradictory. The sceptic who asserts that "no one can know anything" must himself fall foul of this logical axe, since we must ask him how he *knows* that.

Language has now entered the scene. Language is something that marks off man from the ape by a gulf as wide as that stretching from here to the further stars. At least this is true insofar as it affects our thinking about the world and ourselves. That the instincts to eat, drink, copulate, fight, etc., are nearly the same for man and apes cannot alas be doubted; but this is something that could be changing or could, and of course by science, be made to change.

The rational approach of science tells us something about reality. The irrational, or arational it should be called, tells us something too. How do these fit together? Are they related like body and mind? Are they related like body and spirit? Are they two aspects of the same thing?

Philosophy once grappled with questions that affected people in their everyday lives and helped them to decide on moral, political and other issues. Reasons could be cited for not copulating with your neighbour's wife. Advice was available which would help you to vote at an election for one candidate rather than another; today philosophy deals with matters of science, logic and language and even ethics and political science in abstract form.

What are ordinary people to do? What are they to think about the world? This problem of being deserted by the philosopher and failing to be convinced by the Church is partly the result of living at a time of specialization where the rate of change is increasing at an ever-greater pace.

One type of answer to one of our problems though can be given. The world we were brought up in from time immemorial was conceived of as static, whether consciously or unconsciously. Our institutions inherited the Platonic rather than Democritan heritage and have asserted implicitly that things do not really change.

We cannot believe, in our heart of hearts, that one day country cricket will not be played in England, or that baseball will not be played in America. It is obvious at the rational level that change does occur, but we are educated in the widest sense, and unconsciously, to believe it does not. If this is so and the rate of change is, in fact, increasing—and who could possibly doubt it—then we are bound to be increasingly out of tune with the times. Such a state of affairs, even in spite of man's enormous adaptability, must prove self-destroying.

We shall be seeing again and again how resistance to change takes place in people, especially among the most successful of people. This is partly as a result of the need for security which operates against change and adaptation.

It is natural that those who are already happy want to stay that way. It is natural for people not to change their state if their state is satisfactory, and furthermore to resist actively attempts to change them. This is why change must come with new

B

generations and must depend greatly on the education and environment which fosters that new generation.

In Britain, of all the so-called civilized countries, change is probably most resisted and for this we can thank above all the tremendous success of the recent past, most of all in the nineteenth century.

The fact that Britain today is probably changing faster than ever before points to the fact that in spite of resistance to change the pressures bringing change are greater than ever. These pressures are in some measure due to the fact that countries no longer live in isolation from each other; politically, economically and through overall world travel and general awareness, thanks to modern communication, the world is becoming more unified. The question is not whether Britain can change—it can and is changing—but whether it can change quickly enough to keep pace with the changing pressure of events.

Partly because its success is more recent, and partly because of its different, more liberal, heritage, the United States of America is more flexible than Britain. Its problems are mainly social and internal and it is its solution to racial integration which is the prototype of the same issue all over the world.

America has often ruthlessly built change into its system under the pressure of such forces as private enterprise. The fact that national baseball sides like the Giants, the Dodgers and the Braves can leave Brooklyn, New York and Milwaukee respectively and go to Los Angeles, San Francisco and Atlanta is no novelty in America, since changes have existed—if not quite on such a large scale—for many years. The idea that British football teams such as Arsenal or Rangers could leave London or Glasgow and go to other cities would merely make the average British football follower laugh incredulously, but perhaps with a note of apprehension. Sport has important psychological and social significance for any community, and analysis of a country's sporting habits is as good a guide to that community as most.

The past, the present and the future provide the dimensions of change. Sport in the modern formal sense hardly existed in the world a hundred years ago, and certainly professional game players in the sense we know them today did not exist at all.

Sport in the past was mainly for the rich and meant hunting, shooting and fishing, and although it still exists in this form, it is now even more merely a pastime for the richer people and the farmers. This change is due to the change from country to city life for the bulk of the population.

Football is a game of the city and played originally in the streets of the city. Country life naturally produces country sports, whereas city life, by its very nature, tends to produce formal and more stylized games played in severely circumscribed conditions.

The rise of cities is not new, but is a product of the social way of life. The rise and development of the city underwent a major change with the Industrial Revolution. In Britain, where the Revolution was so closely bound up with communication links such as railways and canals, and with power sources such as coal and rivers, the cities became large sprawling centres of concentration. We glimpse here even in a few brief paragraphs something of the complex interrelated nature of social evolution. Lewis Mumford has clearly stated for us one of our main points:

> "Our capacity for effective physical organization has enormously increased; but our ability to create a harmonious counterpoise to these external linkages by means of co-operative and civic associations on both a regional and a world-wide basis, like the Christian Church in the Middle Ages, has not kept pace with these mechanical triumphs."

This is even truer today, more than thirty years after Mumford wrote these words, because of another world war which has intervened, and which has as a result set formal Christian religion even nearer to its final eclipse. What, though, has emerged to take the place of Christianity, where formal Christian beliefs are manifestly weakening? And what replacement is needed, if any?

Society is in evolution; it is changing as circumstances and people change. Evolution emphasizes the survival of those fittest to survive. This does not mean that those who survive are ideal in some sense, only that their organization—whether physiological or social—is sufficient to allow of their existence.

Treating such a view as a statement of what occurs in the world is to say nothing about morality, or what *ought* to occur by some yardstick. What may survive as the best may be completely distasteful to us.

An example could be the complete success of an utterly ruthless and selfish system—Nazi Germany might easily have been, and could still be, such an example. There is nothing in social evolutionary theory that suggests that it is the intrinsically evil nature of Nazism that creates its own destruction. At least this is one of the questions we must answer, especially when we read "Nazi world" for "Nazi Germany".

Our own ideas, of course, as to what is "morally good or bad" are derived largely from the society in which we have lived, so these too are capable of adaptation; we are on quicksand rather than bedrock once more. Always we find we are imposing our own standards on the world, and then rediscovering them and failing to recognize where they originated.

Our difficulties in understanding man's problems in trying to control his own evolution stem from a number of causes. One is as we have said "the problem of various viewpoints". We tend too easily to put blinkers on our own thinking. Traditions are illustrative of this, and while they have a place in any society they must be capable of evolving too; if they become fossilized then the society which owns them is bankrupt and defunct, or will shortly become so.

Another difficulty we have mentioned is that of dimensions. We cannot easily deal with ideas which are not close to our experience, and this is part of the difficulty of not being able to get outside ourselves and look in at the complete system.

We may be mere puffs of smoke on an infinite horizon or a community living in a small bottle floating on a vast ocean. Our sense of space and time is governed by our immediate experience and our span of life.

We live by control and communication. We must communicate to control, and communication has had its fair share of development. Here the future is clearer, and the next phase leads to the colonization of space on the one hand and the complete information transmitter on the other. This second development will have the most detailed reconstruction of the past as part of its function.

We cannot live in Cromwell's time in the sense that we cannot go back in time any more than we can travel faster than light, but we can reconstruct the necessary sensory experience, which makes the question of actually going back irrelevant. Human beings, by using those quickly developing capacities which make them more like gods and less like animals, can reconstruct any event whatever. The capacities of the imagination, involving consciousness, dreaming and almost unlimited suggestibility, are the materials which we shall use.

The adaptability is a part of our basic feedback system at work. Acts giving pleasure are repeated whenever possible, and pain is avoided whenever possible; the masochist calls pain pleasure, but his rule of use is the same. It is conceivable in the end that it is in the imagination that man's quest for happiness could be made complete. But to understand exactly what this means and how the quest is bound up with the evolution of society involves us, as we have already said, in the most deatiled examination of a number of subjects. We must look at science and scientific methods, which lead us automatically to logic and language.

We have already sufficiently emphasized the critical relevance of education, not just at schools and universities, but at every turn of our lives and for the emotions as well as the power to reason. To motivate, to suggest and to imagine—the arts could hardly be avoided here; the arts have always tried to work their magic on us, and sometimes if only in brief spells they have succeeded.

Sex is fundamental to our understanding of people and society; its changing role is one of the things that could most alter our society, even by the end of the century.

As the principal science involved, cybernetics must be discussed in some detail and this means we have to understand just a little about computers and automation.

Finally, we have religion. Religion could be an amalgam of all the other things we have discussed, but we are thinking of religion as an integrating principle—a bed of rock to set into the quicksand. Whether Christianity, or any other existing religion, can survive depends in part on how much the new version of Christianity is acceptable as Christian as opposed to humanism. One's experience and one's feelings do not encourage optimism, but at least we should look and see.

Somehow, though, some formula has to emerge; some social cement has to be found, some groundwork is needed for the imagination to work upon. Science remains the means, and religion or its equivalent is important in supplying some imaginative purpose to the end.

The world of 2000 will be a world which is different from the present world because it can manipulate physical and chemical things with a dexterity which would leave us breathless and which it will take for granted.

What will be just as significant is the extent to which our capacity for language, for thinking and for imagining will have developed—to a state which makes the present day seem like a kindergarten viewed from the Olympian heights of the university.

3 What Science is About

"To follow knowledge like a sinking star
Beyond the utmost bounds of human thought."

"Ulysses"
Tennyson

"The danger of a broad view is that it is often a shallow view."
"The Philosophy of Physical Science"
A. S. Eddington

THE PURSUIT OF SCIENCE is a curiosity in itself. People have an innate sense of curiosity, which makes them wish to acquire knowledge. Even if that knowledge is dangerous or undesirable, the fact is that human beings still wish to discover more and more facts and also wish to express opinions, in abundance; sometimes they confuse the two.

The discovery of facts is much like the lower form of instinctive human development, since animals exhibit exactly the same behaviour. If we place a rat in a new cage or a new maze or any other novel situation, its first response is to walk round the case, nosing at each nook and cranny until it apparently knows exactly what the new circumstances are. This is highly rational behaviour because it means that to *know* the circumstances in which one is placed is to be able to know what to expect in such circumstances. This is exactly why we, as human beings, in the search for security, try to resist change. Black clouds usually mean rain, and to know this is to increase our chance of keeping dry and it also makes us feel secure. Change is, of course, the antithesis of a predictable world; it is a world where prediction is made that much more difficult.

Psychologically, it is now "old hat" to say that children need security above all else. Certainly it is true and true for reasons which are self-evident since security is really the ability to predict the environment, coupled, of course, with the need—an emotional facet—for being wanted; this is a form of hedonism. Love is a vital part of that security; a part of that want. To be looked after by someone who loves you is to be made secure, because both the emotions as well as the reason of the guardian are involved.

What is less obvious but equally true is that adults need security just as much as children. They too are unsettled, even unnerved, by the unpredictable, the unexpected and the unfamiliar; they dislike change. Science provides the answer to this; science provides a method for efficient prediction and this generates a greater measure of control of the environment. But it also accelerates the very fact of and need for change itself, by providing new discoveries which can, and sometimes must, be exploited by the human race, either because they fulfil a vital need, in the case of penicillin for example, or because they are of special use, such as in the case of brainwashing; morality gives way to pragmatism.

Science plays the role then of supplying the means to allow us to achieve our emotional ends, the ends most often being safety and survival, release from pain and the hedonistic pursuit of pleasure. That science may not serve sufficiently as a means, let alone as an end, has been recorded movingly by one of the greatest of the world's scientists, as well as philosopher, Bertrand Russell, who said:

> "Three passions, simple but overwhelmingly strong, have governed my life; the longing for love, the search for knowledge, and unbearable pity for the suffering of mankind. These passions, like great winds, have blown me hither and thither in a wayward course, over a deep ocean of anguish, reaching to the very verge of despair.
>
> I have sought love, first because it brings ecstasy—ecstasy so great I would often have sacrificed all the rest of life for a few hours of this joy . . ."

Russell as a scientist in the very broadest sense is a man speaking both logically and with great clarity of understanding and feeling; he is a man who understands clearly that life is more than science and science is to be used as a servant to humanity. The rub is, of course, that to control science means to understand it and this we have, as a community, yet to achieve.

When we do, we have an even more difficult problem to solve, the means of controlling science itself. Science as a method can produce results that could allow us one day literally to change the shape of our universe, so our problem is to provide a sort of superscience which will be both dynamic and capable of harbouring such a potential god, or devil, or both in one. It must be a science to control science.

The history of science is bound to be relevant to our search just as all history is relevant to us as a basis for extrapolation for the future. Henry Ford's statement that "history is bunk" can be taken to mean that we are not to feel shackled by our past; this is the spirit of the pioneer. But history, like all experience, is the only possible basis for making statements as to the nature of the future. In trying to learn from history, we must try always to remember "the problem of dimensions".

The Greeks played a very vital role in the history of science even though on the whole they were not scientific; they thought of science in its pure form as a puzzle in logic. Their geometry and mathematics generally was an exercise in mental agility rather than a part of the process of trying to explain the world in which they lived. Anaxagoras was one of the exceptions to this statement and represented, as did Democritus, another exception, what we would today call a scientific viewpoint. He was, though, threatened with death for his views, and such was the prejudice of the times that he was widely regarded as being mad for believing the sun to be larger than the Peloponnesus. Indeed for such a heretical, although as we now know true, statement, he all but lost his life.

Tradition is something which by its very meaning correctly fixed the old static or very slowly changing attitudes of a changing civilization. The tradition of knowledge has been born in Egypt and Mesopotamia prior to its emergence in Greece as culture. In the Near East it emerged in the development of industrial arts. The Greeks in general were cultural theorists and not people to soil their hands by applying their ideas to practical problems.

Rome supplied some practical scientific application in its contribution to the history of prescience and there followed a long fallow period leading to the Middle Ages, which saw a revival of scientific interest.

In the twelfth century, it was the growth of trade that accompanied the revival of learning and partly caused it. Towns grew and water power spread and the magnetic compass and the clock were developed. Technology was really evolving and with it, as Lewis Mumford has pointed out, a change of heart from the monastic speculations about eternity to the real world of space and time. Our next state in evolution will be partly a reversal of this procedure, but at a far more complex level, which makes speculation and contemplation features of great practical importance in the real world, the world of practicality.

One important feature of learning is the fact that human beings lack the capacity to keep all the information they need at any one time in their heads, or even in their libraries. Although the key to "the universal knowledge machine" lies in keeping in the head information about where to find the necessary information externally, this is of little use without the ability to use the information or even know that you need it in the first instance. The age of superspecialization is with us and it is from these bonds we shall escape by the communal use of man and machines. By putting our resources together, we can become superpeople; we can literally become, as an individual in an organized group, several hundred times more powerful than any *one* present brain working in isolation.

Leonardo da Vinci had even less help in his work than later scientists, and neither did he find anyone to publish his works for him, as Halley did for Sir Isaac Newton. But both of these geniuses operated over domains of information that were tiny compared with the amount of knowledge available today, which will be even tinier when compared with our knowledge at the end of the century.

In the history of science, we continually see its development going hand in hand with technological development. Without the microscope biology could never have developed in the way it has, and the same applies to astronomy and the telescope. Even the truth of abstract theories such as the theory of relativity could not have been confirmed without such equipment, and indeed the two experimental physicists Michaelson and Morley played a vital part as the essential background to the maturing of Einstein's ideas.

The fact that in mathematics the calculus was independently developed by Leibniz and Newton is a reminder that most scientific advances are not matters of chance, but depend upon meeting the needs of society at some particular point in its development.

The discovery of the atomic theory in physics and chemistry, the theories of evolution in biology, the increased understanding of ecology or the interaction of species and their environment, the arrival of even more mathematical techniques culminating in the computer, are milestones which are to be seen as a gradual unfolding of knowledge, an ever-increasing process which changes the face of whole worlds, and even itself.

The idea that the world is a material thing is not, perhaps surprisingly, very old. Pledge put it this way:

> "We sometimes speak as if this (a material thing) was the 'lowest' and perhaps by implication, the most primitive of our ideas—this of a material something existing independently of the observer and underlying, essentially unchanged, the changes and varieties of matter, such as fusion, solution, chemical reaction. But in fact this idea, so far as science goes, has been only slowly and recently formed . . ."

We have certainly made the idea of material things yield enormous dividends, and now are about to move into a world where, without in any sense abandoning the notions of science, we are forced to see that explanation, prediction and the methods of science do not provide for all the needs of humanity; paradoxically, it needs science to make such a point really clear. It is scientific method that provides the vital link between the past and the future.

Scientific *method* is above all that which is changing the face of our society. Naturally, in saying this we are not necessarily saying that the change is for the better, because we do not know what "better" means in such a context, if it means anything at all.

One of our themes, though, is that what happens to be the case—what is true—is *not* necessarily what we want or what is good for us. Not that we always rationalize the good from our needs, but this is without doubt one of the gifts possessed by human beings. So let us now simply try to understand what scientific method is about without attempting to evaluate it. At this moment the method and the results are all we are concerned about. We should, though, bear in mind what it implies for social evolution.

Science entails the systematic collecting of data in order to allow systematic improvement in performance as a result of having the latest available information, while trying wherever possible to understand the principles involved in its use.

Science as a method applies, or can be applied, to anything at all. If I go out to do some shopping and I know that it is early-closing day in the northern half of the town, but not in the southern half, I know, as a result, that if I want to buy goods of most kinds I go to the southern half. However, I also know that there are certain exceptions to these rules. For example, the newspaper shops and the confectioners are open every day; my behaviour will now depend on what I want to buy.

The principle involved is clear. You have a goal or purpose, and you need information to enable you to *predict* as to that purpose; science enables you to do just this.

We sometimes have difficulties because some of the information we need is highly specific, although sometimes, on the other hand, it is quite general. In other words, sometimes we want to know whether Mr. Smith is opening his leather goods shop, and sometimes we want to know where *any* leather goods shop is open, not necessarily Mr. Smith's.

So we proceed to pick up information, to acquire it from all sorts of sources, expecially from other people and from direct observation of the events. "Seeing is believing" is a well-established belief, but it is sometimes particularly inaccurate, as testimony experiments show. A student had been instructed to act out a role in a fake laboratory experiment. The experimenter himself has a mass of complicated apparatus arranged for what was alleged to be a public demonstration of a certain experiment. Many hundreds of students were watching in a large lecture theatre as the demonstration was about to start.

The moment before the demonstration starts, the apparatus is knocked off the test bench and smashes into small pieces. At the same moment as this apparatus is knocked off, in fact intentionally by the demonstrator, the student who had been planted for the purpose of deceiving the class gets to his feet and walks over to the table where the apparatus is standing.

After the experimental demonstration had been abandoned, the students who saw, or claimed to have seen, what happened were asked detailed questions, and they universally blamed the "planted" student.

The reason for this is obvious enough. "Seeing is not believing" so much as "believing is seeing". What you expect to happen or what you think must have happened is what you say and think actually did happen.

There are thousands of examples which make it clear that what we perceive, or say we perceive, may be inaccurate because of the difficulty we all have in separating the actual sensory experience, the photograph in visual terms, from the implications of the occurrence. One further experiment which should be mentioned here is that which gets two people to give independent accounts of the same football match. Provided they are not told in advance that they are to be asked to describe the game, and provided they are respectively fairly dedicated supporters of the two different teams, then their accounts are laughably different. Quite frequently, even professional sports reporters in the press report the game quite differently from each other, and any spectator will know the experience of subsequently reading an account of a match he has seen and being quite amazed at what the reporter seems to have seen.

An experiment was carried out along these lines in an American college football match between Princeton and Dartmouth, and the different interpretations of certain incidents involving rough play were extraordinarily, even humorously, different. It need hardly be said that the Dartmouth supporters blamed the fouls on the Princeton team and *vice versa*.

The power of suggestion is the immensely powerful factor we are drawing attention to, the harnessing of which could place us nearer to our next goals than the search for objectivity.

Scientists know a good deal about the subjective element in observation. Many years ago the idea of "the personal equation" grew up in the domain of astronomy. Indeed it grew up in the world of the Astronomer Royal at Greenwich precisely because different observers were found to have different speeds of response.

There is no science without the observer, and no observer who can be sure he records only what is independent of himself. We do not in the end even know whether other people think, or even exist, except as figments of our imaginings. We are all tiny ants on some dunghill remote in a small fragment of the universe. Our universe is but a puff of smoke in space and in time, or at least it may be so and we cannot *know* for certain whether it is or not.

To try to eliminate subjective error, scientists normally take the average of a number of readings and always try to get a consensus of opinion. They insist that all experiments are repeatable using *any* sane observer, and they insist that all the evidence used is publicly testable; this is the best we can do to eliminate subjectivity. Someone sooner or later inevitably objects to science when it gets to the point where observations cannot be made directly, and this happens when, for example, we try to reconstruct the structure of the atomic nucleus. We use models for this purpose and these models can be used to provide a mechanism—or a blueprint for a mechanism—which does what we want.

This is a purely practical matter; there is nothing to stop us pretending the inside of a clock is a football field with footballers playing, *if* the analogy helps to provide a correct prediction about football.

We have to be careful not to think that, when we go beyond our ability to observe, that which we posit as consistent with what we observe really exists in such a form. God as a *person* is possibly such an example of what we mean.

Metaphysics is the name sometimes given to speculative science, where direct evidence is hardly applicable. Since any statement in any language stating any fact about the world must necessarily be liable to error, we should not make too big an issue of this graduation from science to metaphysics.

Scientific method attempts to collect information and regard it as factual if there is good evidence for believing it, and then to make inferences from that evidence. Any event which happens repeatedly in the same way, or nearly so, illustrates the approach.

Consider what we call public houses in Britain, or bars as they are more often called in America. Suppose we observe the behaviour of the owners of such worthy establishments. We start, say, in England and watch simply their hours of opening and closing. You notice straightaway the relatively abstracted nature of our problem. We do not care whether the barman is tall or short, and although we may care that the barmaids are attractive, this is not relevant to our current very abstract problem.

We cannot sensibly ask the publican himself when he opens and closes his pub. He may not tell us the truth since many people say one thing and actually do another, even sometimes without knowing it, but in any case if we asked a question the analogy with the greater part of science would break down. After all, the chemist cannot sensibly ask the powdered mixture in his test-tube about its own chemical constituents. If he did he would not get an answer and if heard would certainly be regarded as mad.

We observe and note what we observe. There are two or three of us doing the observing to avoid subjective mistakes and to minimize the power of suggestion. We find that the bar opens at 10.30 a.m. and closes at 2.30 p.m., and then again in the evening it starts again at 5.30 p.m. and closes at 10.30 p.m.

We find the pattern is almost the same every day. In fact it is not quite the same because Sunday has different hours. On Sunday the hours are 12.00 to 2.00 p.m., and then 7.00 to 10.00 p.m. So our corrected pattern is the above for six days and the modified one on Sunday.

We are, as scientists, pleased that our problem has proved such an easy one to solve. We can use a simple deductive argument and say that if each week is the same, and we are still checking on that, then given that today is Friday, I can tell you exactly at what times the pub will open and at what time it will shut.

But now something else has happened; our tests are showing that the inductive part of the argument is not correct after all. Every week is not, in fact, the same as every other week. On public holidays—although as an abstract observer we may not know the name for these special occasions—we have an extension and sometimes the pub will behave as if it were a Sunday when it is in fact Friday.

We were aware from the start that there were difficulties because all publicans or bartenders did not open the bar on time and certainly often failed to shut them on time.

Should we now shift our ground and say that our first pattern is wrong? The answer to this is obviously "yes", because we are using this inductively derived pattern as a basis for our whole argument. We must clearly look carefully at both inductive and deductive arguments, but at least at this stage we can say that induction is a type of guess, and we hope it is an intelligent and accurate guess; deduction is a process of drawing out the consequences of our induction or guesses. We often say logic is deduction, but even here there is some confusion over words, since Sherlock Holmes often talked of deduction when he meant induction.

While we make asides about the processes of drawing inferences—or logic, as we call it—we are still awaiting a new guess about the opening and closing times of bars.

If you take a trip from London to New York at this stage, your disillusionment may be complete. The bars there have very different times. The first impression is that you can drink around the clock; all twenty-four hours of the day is possible drinking time. All that you have learned in England seems now to be wasted.

In fact, of course, there are still specific hours kept by most bars and there are certain hours, especially between four in the morning and about ten, when you cannot drink at the vast majority of bars. It takes, in fact, a canny New Yorker to bar-map his way through the whole twenty-four hours of a day.

But worse is to follow because you will find Atlanta, Georgia, is totally "dry" on a Sunday and Prince Edward Island in Canada is (or certainly was) totally dry all the time.

On returning, dispirited, to England, you can at least console yourself with the thought that prediction will pay off better there, precisely because you have a better model, or map, of England. On a train journey across America you can suddenly have your whisky removed from under your nose as you cross a state line, and then you can have beer only, or just coffee. Then a few hours later it is "free for all" again and all this can happen on the same train journey. In Britain if the trains have drinks at all you are always able to get them, and you can have brandy with your breakfast kippers if you wish.

We can now see clearly the problem. If you study only the pubs in Beaconsfield, say, and they vary to some extent, you cannot necessarily apply the same rules to the rest of England, although they would turn out in fact to be a fairly good guide. The same rules do not help, though, when applied to America or France, or most other European countries.

Statisticians come in here and say that you can only talk sensibly (scientifically) and make predictions about the domains you have actually sampled. The trouble is that we have, by necessity, only sampled, and we use average times or some such statistical measure of the hours of opening and closing. Another trouble is that we cannot be sure the whole system will not suddenly change, and in any case our model—this is what scientists sometimes call a theory—is not 100 per cent accurate because of public holidays and special extensions at holiday times.

One issue we must be absolutely clear about. If it were not for the fact of having a pattern of repetition we could not predict with any accuracy at all. A pattern of repetition is sometimes called periodic, or since it is not quite precisely repetitive, we call it almost periodic. It is in fact sufficiently periodic to allow prediction.

If you can predict events you may also be able to control them. If you can control events you are in a very powerful position. It is precisely the increase in that control wherein lies the dramatic power of science.

We have to add that controlling the environment does not necessarily mean understanding it. Many of us learn to restart a radio or television by shaking it or banging it on the side. Psychiatrists know that the destruction of some of the tissues of the frontal lobes of the brain alleviates certain anxiety states. It does not follow on this account that they understand why the desired effect is achieved.

By 'understanding' here we really mean the ability to map out (or model) the whole mechanism, so that you know that a particular external movement or a particular chemical treatment will have just "this" or "that" effect on the system.

Understanding the principles of a system means more still. It means, for example, that you understand how things like clocks work and almost all clocks have the same—or some of the same—principles involved in their construction.

You could perhaps say also of hearts that they are all constructed on more or less the same principle, even if some have three chambers and some have four. Aircraft are similar to each other, too, even if some are vast jets like Concorde and others are piston-driven biplanes like the Tiger Moth.

As a scientist you observe features of the world and abstract certain things which are relevant to setting up a particular theory. You construct a model and predict from the model to the actual world. And when the prediction fails you adjust your model to more nearly fit the facts. This is the adjustment you make in our bar-cum-pub example in changing from a seven-day to a 365-day cycle (try to forget about leap year).

Some people have taken maps, as we have already hinted, as good examples of models. If the map has the same structure and relationships as the territory it maps, then prediction can be excellent. If the structures are different then prediction will be poor and we shall change our map, since clearly we do not want, even if we can, to change the territory. This, though, may be true of some aspects of science; the psychiatrist's job is precisely that of changing the territory, where in the analogy the territory is some sick person's behaviour.

As far as maps are concerned, note the feature of abstracting. You extract and highlight different features if your map is for the airman than if it is for the motorist or the canal-user. Always we abstract features for our modelling relevant to some particular purpose.

Observation is not only vital to the collecting of the information from which we make our induction (some generalization or guess), it is also vital to confirming or otherwise the rightness of our resulting model.

We fly over the Falkland Islands and observe their shape and draw a rough map and hand it over to our seafaring friends. They use it to navigate the island and they fill in more detail as it is needed, making small corrections here and there and generally improving all the time on its predictive capacity. Because we drew the map from the air we may well not have bothered with features such as underwater rocks or wrecks which may be vital to the ship if not to the aircraft. If these features are not carefully checked before use, we may lose some ships before the maps become sufficiently good. The danger is that we may even lose all our ships. It is exactly the same with the human predicament. If we do not plan ahead for these increasingly changing times we must inevitably fail to survive.

We have come now to logic and language. These are both critical abilities which are not, over and above a trivial amount, available to any other species than man. Without the context of the scientific method we have mentioned the two logical methods of deduction and induction; let us now clarify what we mean by these methods.

Deduction is the ability to draw conclusions from what you know. If there are more people in New York than there are hairs on any person's head it follows by deductive logic that at least two people in New York have the same number of hairs on their head.

One is as hesitant about explaining logical inferences as one is about explaining jokes. Let us take some simple numbers to explain our point. If there are 6 million people in New York and the most hairy-headed man or woman in New York has $5\frac{1}{2}$ million hairs, then some people must have the same number of hairs. We can allocate o hairs to one man, 1 hair to the next, 2 to the next, and so on. But when we get to the $5\frac{1}{2}$ millionth person then he or she *must* have one of the numbers already allocated, i.e. between o and $5\frac{1}{2}$ million, so the argument holds. There must be at least $\frac{1}{2}$ million duplicates or some other sort of repeats.

Suppose you were told the argument in Swahili, and let us assume that you do not understand Swahili. Under these circumstances, you could not possibly see the compelling nature of the argument. But even if told the argument in English and you did not understand what was meant by a key word such as "more" then you would still fail to appreciate the force of the argument. If you thought "more" meant *less*, for example, then the argument would be absurd. A simpler deductive argument underlines the point. "I live in Bath and Bath is in Somerset", therefore I can conclude that "I live in Somerset". But if I do not understand what the words "live in" mean I would not be able to understand the logic of the argument, nor draw an appropriate conclusion.

Deductive arguments depend on an understanding of what the words used mean. Furthermore they are in a sense telling you what the consequence of that meaning is.

Inductive reasoning is more or less the opposite in that it argues from the particular to the general as opposed to arguing from the general to the particular. I see eight dogs in succession which are all Alsatians so I may conclude inductively—and quite wrongly, of course—that all dogs are Alsatians. The mistake here illustrates the point that we can never be certain about such inductive generalizations; we should be in a position to check them by observations. This is one of the problems of science. We say in science you should only talk about that which you can observe, and it is for this very reason of observation being the basis of our whole argument; sometimes, of course, we use such devices as "observable in principle" or "indirectly observable", but we are always then on dangerous ground. Metaphysics is speculative precisely because it describes and discusses the non-observable.

This last sentence tells us one clearcut thing about the meaning of the word "speculative". It refers to something which is not capable of being tested by observation. Some people would as a result argue that it is not testable at all.

Put our inductive statements to a test and you see that whatever test you make, it can never be *completely beyond doubt*. "All doves are grey" is an inductive generalization. But suppose you saw twenty million doves and they were all grey, would you be sure on that account that *all* doves were grey? The main trouble is that you could never be sure that you had seen every dove. You could, of course, also be mistaken about the colour you think you see.

One worse howler is to define the word "dove" to include the property of being grey. If you then look around the world and see a "green dove" it cannot be a dove, because you have said doves are necessarily grey. You must, it is clear, only test statements that are capable of being shown to be false. If there is not such a possibility, the test immediately becomes pointless.

Logic and science are clearly closely related: like Goneril and Regan to some, like Abelard and Heloise to others. But whatever you think of logic and science, they are related, and very closely related.

Another relative of the same family, perhaps Cordelia, is language. Language is the key to communication. Without language we as a species could not have accumulated information from generation to generation since without language each generation would virtually start again from scratch. So important is language that we always have to be aware of its pitfalls, its vagueness and its ambiguity.

We can give one quick and simple illustration of litmus test we should always bear in mind. Someone tells you "the world is oval" and you do not know for certain whether he is wrong (or you are) about *the facts* or whether he does not understand (or you don't) what *the word* "oval" means. It could be either, so further questions are needed which may, or may not, clear the matter up. Even explanations or definitions use other words as their basic material, and some of these may be vague, and so a whole chain of misunderstanding can be set up.

The other two litmus tests are the questions "What do you mean?" and "How do you know?", to be used sparingly on the innocent, and only when really necessary to the eliciting of information.

So language and logic are vital to the future as they have been to the whole development of man, and they are the keystones to the development of science.

The future will see dramatic changes in science, not primarily in principle but in methods. The change of principle that will occur is to broaden attitudes of science, especially to the social sciences, and psychology which will pave the way for this broadening process in general terms. 'Mind', if we can use the word discretely (words are sometimes written in single quotation marks to remind us that we are talking of the word itself), applies to part of what emerges from organism, and is related to it as the performance of an automobile is to its structure, such as number of cylinders, etc. 'Mind' is the source of imagination and the highest creative capacities of human beings. The fact that it is the performance of a mechanism, be it ever so complicated, should not obscure the fact of its tremendous power.

Minds can be and will be produced artificially—this is what cybernetics is about—but the mind's capacity, whether artificial or natural born human being, is vital to the future. We must therefore broaden our scientific canvas from the purely materialistic explanatory concepts to other concepts where questions are asked and answers required. This refers to feelings of love and hate, of needs and longings, of moments of ecstasy and vivid imaginings. And sometimes it is not a matter of question and answer at all, but the feeling of certitude, the holding of faith, the longing for love, which may be explicable in rational terms, but may yet not be the explanation that we seek.

As is obvious, the communication channels of the year 2000 will be vastly different from those of the present. Newspapers will be a thing of the past with but a few exceptions. News will travel through satellite by full sensory communication and the observer who is plugged into the message source will have the full emotional and full sensory feelings of the originator and not merely the abstracted facts as conveyed by language.

We talk to each other to give each other information and to persuade other people of the correctness of our views. But words are vague and imprecise and are better suited to poetic than to logical use. If we could share other people's direct experience, we could then get rid of that vagueness. We shall be able to do this in stages. First by simulation of taste, smell, etc., and then by actually plugging in to another person's nervous system. This is a vital part of future development.

All of this will be done by science for humanity and could not be stopped even if we all agreed that it was undesirable, and this is all due to human curiosity.

Massive interconnected interstellar data banks with individual links to all parts of the galaxy are inevitable. Communication systems with any degree of reality required will be set up. The reconstruction of the past is a major task to be undertaken and the complete picture of the present preserved for all time, and this is precisely a part of this control of sensation. The future too must be increasingly predictable; the notion of time has now changed in our very grasp.

4 Machines, Computers and Games

> "The West has got to help in this transformation. The trouble is the West with its divided culture finds it hard to grasp just how big, and above all just how fast, the transformation must be."
> *"The Two Cultures: and a Second Look"*
> C. P. Snow

> "Most of our daily activities are carried on without reflection, and it seldom occurs to us to question that which generally passes as true."
> *"An Introduction to Logic"*
> M. Cohen and E. Nagel

THE HISTORY OF SCIENCE has some clearcut messages for us, and none clearer than the fact that a few people have, almost from the beginning of recorded human thought, considered human beings to be nothing more nor less than complex machines. This may be obvious to people of the next century, but it is certainly not obvious to us in this.

Democritus was an early Greek philosopher whose work was at its peak in about 420 BC, and who was, like his contemporary, Leucippus, an enemy of the sophists. The sophists we should identify primarily with Plato and Aristotle. Their greatness, though undoubted, has nevertheless had the effect of holding up the development of scientific thinking as we know it today.

Democritus is justly famous precisely because his views were at least representative of a school which was essentially scientific. His work anticipated the modern atomic view of matter and he had a mechanical interpretation of motion which was correct —by modern physical standards—in all essentials. Parmenides and others of about the same time also had a "scientific" view of the world but all of them lacked the methods and the equipment to do more than conjecture about the nature of reality.

It was partly for this reason and partly because of the dominance of emotive idealistic and poetic thinking that it was Plato and Aristotle whose views had the greatest impact on our society from that time on, almost until the present day; science was still a long way off.

Perhaps no Greek actually said in so many words that humans were machines, but many were inclined to that point of view. By the eighteenth century, however, we find a whole group of philosophers who held just such a view. Diderot, Helvetius and La Mettrie were members of the movement and their influence was very extensive. Helvetius in particular directly influenced Jeremy Bentham and James Mill, father of John Stuart Mill. Their problem was still, even in a world where science was gathering momentum, that of producing evidence for their beliefs. No one, though, did anything to show in practice how it could actually be that man was a sort of machine.

The development of the digital computer by Charles Babbage, that unusually eccentric English genius, represents one major advance which provided some evidence that man is something like a machine *of some kind*. Babbage's work during the early part of the nineteenth century was pioneer work which led directly to the construction of the modern digital computer.

In the digital computer we have a machine which most of its originators saw either as providing a mechanical means of doing mathematics or as providing a means of handling data such as accounts, invoices and suchlike paperwork, and it has performed, in this particular role, a large part of what we talk of as automation. The originators did not primarily think of human beings as being machinelike, only that machines could be made to do *some* of the things that humans can do.

Another approach to such "intelligent" machines was through mathematics, since some mathematicians tried to show that all of mathematics could be formulated as a postulational (or axiomatic) system. Readers whose only recent contact with mathematics was the geometry of Euclid will doubtless recall the system whereby theorems were proved by showing them to be consistent with certain postulates (or axioms) which were assumed.

The controversy still exists in mathematics as to whether all of mathematics can be reduced to postulates, but there is now some evidence that it cannot. Let us explain straightaway what this has to do with human beings being machinelike.

If we have a set of postulates and all the theorems of mathematics follow from the postulates, they provide a mechanical or machinelike means for describing the subject. In fact, we can argue that all mathematicians are machinelike in some sense; we can even argue that a sufficiently complicated machine such as a computer could do all of mathematics for us.

There is a further point here. Mathematics is often quite rightly thought of as one of man's highest intellectual achievements, so that if mathematics can be performed by machines, just what, we might ask, is there that cannot be performed by machines?

Here we have to define the word 'machinelike' a little more carefully. 'Machinelike' means that virtually no intelligence is needed to carry through a process. So if it is suggested that mathematics is machinelike one can understand the mathematician's reservations about, not to say downright opposition to, such a suggestion.

If I ask how many people are on the electoral roll of a city like Leeds, I can count them and say what the total is. This is surely machinelike and can obviously be done on a computer since computers can certainly count.

In fact, let us say that 'machinelike' means capable of being done on a computer; then we need to discover what, if anything, cannot be done on a computer. This is precisely one of the issues with which the science of cybernetics is concerned. We shall be talking about cybernetics as such in chapter 5, so we will not anticipate how far that science has progressed to date except insofar as it affects our understanding of man as a machine and our understanding of computers and what they can and cannot do.

Computers are simple in principle, just as a motor car is simple in principle. A motor car has an engine that provides power to rotate the wheels and move the whole vehicle including the engine in the direction steered by the driver. The details of the electrical circuitry which provides lights, horn, spark for igniting the petrol (in a gaslike state) in the cylinders of the car, and the hydraulic system, the suspension, and the like all make the whole picture very much more complicated in practice. The practical details are considerable but the principles are simple, and so it is with the computer.

For those who use hand calculators it may be of some help to say that a computer is much like a hand calculator. The only difference is that the movements of fingers and hand, pressing the buttons and cranking the handle, are now coded and placed into the store of the machine. This makes it *automatic* and able to carry on independently for long periods of time without human interference.

For convenience, and to allow of great speed, all modern computers are also electronic. The result is that they can add up numbers many thousands of times faster than a human being can. We have already made this point about speed in our discussion of dimensions in chapter 2.

The computer has information put into it, it then performs the steps of the computation and finally can output the information for human use.

The input is simply a matter of placing information in coded form on to a sheet of paper and placing it into the reading head of the computer. It is then translated into its internal code which is usually represented by switches. To get an idea of how this occurs imagine a pianola, which is very similar in principle. Imagine a sheet of paper with ten differently shaped holes punched on it to represent the numbers 0, 1, 2, 3, 4, 5, 6, 7, 8, and 9. Also imagine we can write letters as numbers if we want to, so 1 = A, 2 = B, 3 = C, 4 = D, and so on. We can always keep letters and numbers separate as on a typewriter by having a press-down key which distinguishes small letters (let's pretend these are numbers) from capital letters (these can represent letters).

Now we have a series of instructions to add numbers together to find the square root of numbers or some such thing, and we can type out our input sheets with our special typewriter with no difficulty at all.

So we can summarize the process of getting the information into our computer. We write out all the necessary instructions and all the numbers needed in the correct order—and this is called computer programming. We then take our special typewriter to type out the program (the set of instructions and data) on a long sheet of paper tape which is now covered with holes like a pianola roll.

We take the roll to the computer and put it on to a spool and feed the tape under a reader. This simply translates the holes into electrical pulses which change the state of the internal switches of the computer.

If you are playing the game of imagining, the best way is to imagine the inside of the computer is made up of thousands of tiny electric switches—indeed this is exactly the situation.

You have to imagine several million switches inside the computer, and this is where the electronic experts come in, providing miniature circuits wherein you can have millions of barely visible switches inside a box about the size of a radiogram. It is nearly down to the size of a human brain; but it is still big, and cannot yet do as much.

The cost of computers is perhaps as important as their potential, and the universality of computers in the future will depend on that cost. There is little doubt that the present computer—costing perhaps £1,000,000—will in twenty years' time cost no more than £10,000 and could cost far less. The computer of tomorrow, which will be a hundred times more powerful, will cost, say, £50,000. It is important continually to remind ourselves that in the next thirty years we shall achieve, scientifically, more than in the last *million* years, which means in effect more than the whole history of man to date.

The output of the computer is just like a printer, typewriter or teleprinter, and reverses, in effect, the input. In principle we have a simple system but we need to say a word or two about the internal operations. We are imagining switches, millions of them, all representing letters or numbers. The basic arithmetical operation to be performed is that of adding numbers. The reason that this is basic is because almost all of mathematics can be reduced to this in the end. Subtraction is addition using negative numbers. Multiplication is repeated addition and division is a form of multiplication. Even more complex mathematics can mostly be reduced, sometimes by long and detailed arguments, to the addition of something, even if the something is sometimes a little odd, like logarithms or so-called "irrational" numbers. Always, though, it is essentially the operation of addition that is required.

The performance of addition on a computer is like that of a cyclometer or gas meter; it simply ticks over adding one unit (mile or therm) at a time, and then after 9 the next digit moves up to 10, and 0 starts again through 1, 2 and up to 9. If we want to add two numbers together we simply need a set of sprockets which interlock like a cyclometer or any other counting meter. Add 4 to 5 turns the sprocket four times and then five more times. So if the dial reads 0 originally, it now reads 9. It takes 9/10 of a mile to do this in an automobile mileometer, but the same thing can be done electronically in millionths of a second.

So the computer has arrived, and we can do our sums at speeds totally beyond the imaginings of our forefathers. Clever, even very clever, it certainly is, but what light does this shed on the human mind or human brain?

We can now take a closer look at the question of machine thinking. We must be careful to think of a machine as something which we can construct artificially, not something which is incapable of thinking and has necessarily got no intelligence, which is what we normally mean by the word 'machine'. 'Machine' is not a good choice of term for this reason, but it does at least have impact. If we say that by 'machine' we mean something very different from what is usually meant then we are slightly better off.

If we built a human machine we should certainly need a tremendously complicated blueprint and a far more detailed knowledge of chemistry than we possess in 1970. Simple chemical machines do, however, exist which look like nervous tissues growing together and then growing apart again. These have been made in chemical and electromagnetic fields and are the fore-runners of the laboratory-made human being of the future.

We cannot, of course, say with certainty that machines could be made to think, nor can we be sure that human beings can be made artificially, which is in some ways much the same thing, and we must actually do it if we wish to be sure it can be done and this is precisely what cyberneticians are doing.

This takes us back to those mathematicians who had the idea of making all mathematics machinelike or postulational. They failed in the end, and mathematicians rejoiced and said "Aha, so mathematics *does* require insight and creative skill and such abilities as only human beings possess". The answer to this is "yes", but the follow-up to that is that even though this is true *there is still no reason to doubt that insight and creative skill can be built into a machine*. If you build in the potentialities, then, provided the system is adaptable, it can learn to modify itself as external circumstances change; this is precisely what human beings themselves do.

The blockage, partly emotional, that besets most people when they try to envisage humanlike or superhumanlike machines is one of thinking that what is man-made cannot be better than the maker, but if this were so evolution itself would have proved impossible. In computer terms, we simply underline the term "self-programming". If it is adaptable, it can modify itself and evolve, whether man-made or not, and in any case man himself is man-made, and this we must never forget.

People will ultimately be built in the laboratory but probably not by the year 2000. By 2000 we shall obviously have all the replacement surgery under control and iron lungs will seem as remote to the medical practice of the time as the use of blood-letting is to us now.

The broader issues are clear enough, and we then shall have to face sooner or later the problem of immortality, and that in turn is followed by the problems of being overtaken by the more highly developed species; ironically, this could be a species we ourselves manufacture in the laboratory. The imminence of such results should serve as a warning that we must carefully examine the implications of what scientists do right now, in the short term, let alone in the immediate future. Any failure to anticipate sufficiently or to understand enough, and so far we are nowhere near satisfying either criterion, is bound to spell disaster.

The robots of 2000 will appear as automation but will pervade every aspect of our being—decision-taking, planning, indeed everything that can and will be carried out by a later generation of sets of computers, working together as a society; our job is to pave the way for this and to plan to control it and also to try to control it democratically, if that will mean anything by such a time.

We now pass to a discussion of games. The scene is set by the interrogation game, which makes the point that if you cannot in a question-and-answer game distinguish a man from a machine, then there is no difference at the rational level; for this purpose you are obviously not allowed to hear or see the participants, nor even their handwriting, so every message of the conversation must be typed.

It is vital that we absorb the full implication of the fact that games are models of either real life or abstract situations and it is profitable for the scientist to study them. This means that it is profitable for everyone to study games, and we mean here especially the thinking games rather than the more physical ones.

Physical games are necessary to keep our organic state up to scratch, or to help to do so. In the future such muscular tone and organic wellbeing can be produced by drugs, but this does not necessarily alter the gladiatorial appeal of games. In the age of leisure feats of daring, moments of great physical skill, are likely to prove more sought after than they are at the moment. In this respect the English cricket fan—those few who remain—is hopeful that we shall in the future have the leisure to return to an almost academic study of matches that often last as long as six days.

By simple "thinking games" we mean simple games like snap, noughts-and-crosses or strip Jack naked where relatively little skill is involved, so that a machine procedure is available for noughts-and-crosses which allows anybody to play the game perfectly. This is why at school, when bored by some lesson on Latin, scripture or mathematics, one sought consolation in a game that also turned out to lose its attractions; after a while every game was drawn unless one was distracted into a piece of carelessness or by the interference of a teacher.

Note that snap and strip Jack naked, while also being simple and therefore often dull, have a different property from noughts-and-crosses; they involve a random element or a luck factor.

You are dealt what you hope are well-shuffled cards and such a shuffling destroys any sensible organization of the cards; you are at the beck and call of chance. This, in fact, is the only interesting feature of strip Jack naked, where you simply follow the rule of giving away one card for a Jack, two for a Queen, and so on until one of the players is left with all the cards. Snap has the added ingredient of encouraging quick responding, so that if you do not see the similarities in two cards as quickly as your opponent does, you lose. This means that all of our three simple games are different. Furthermore, there are other differences since noughts-and-crosses is for two persons only, while the other games can be played by two or more players. Anyone who has played "grab" snap with more than two players knows that the consequences can be extremely painful.

There are other games like ludo (or parchesi, as it is some-times called), dominoes, snakes-and-ladders and halma (or Chinese checkers) that show variations on the same patterns as our first three. The use of a single dice or a number of dice is an alternative luck element to the shuffle of cards, and some-times as in monopoly both can be involved, although, of course, monopoly like so many other board games is an obvious simula-tion of a real-life situation and comes nearer to the sort of game in which we are interested as businessmen, planners and scientists.

You can play games which involve coalitions, as is obvious in both auction and contract bridge, for example, and this is a feature that can be added to monopoly, which if played on a larger, more complicated, board with more room for trading, as well as property investment, could provide a very close model to that of a business game. Business games represent an attempt to provide, in the more formal lecture room of a business school, the equivalent of such a "supermonopoly"; they are often, in fact, much easier to play than would appear from the allusion to "supermonopoly".

There is no reason to believe that the playing of such games skilfully is highly correlated with success in thinking. The logician and the mathematician must be capable of being a skilful player of such games, and the more obviously so as we diminish or even eliminate altogether the elements of chance.

This is why games such as draughts (or checkers), and even more so chess, are thought of as the ultimate in the demands they make on game-playing skill.

Games form a base for logical operating. The kind of abstract skill needed to be a world-class mathematician is the kind of ability that the world looks for—or presumably should look for—in its leaders; provided, of course, such people are also worldly and humane.

Some games have played such a vital role in science that a whole branch of mathematics has grown up called "theory of games". This branch of mathematics has been applied particularly to economic behaviour, but applies equally well to any decision-making situation whatever.

This discussion of games should place mathematics in a new light for those unfortunate people who hated every minute of the agony of trying to understand even the simpler parts of algebra and geometry. Mathematics is perhaps the worst taught subject in the world, and certainly most often made the dullest. No-one—or practically no-one—at school glimpses any of the quality of poetry in mathematics or any of the elegance which can be so satisfying.

The equation of beauty and truth is not a new one, and the problem posed is that the concept of beauty is difficult to pin down. It is not so much that there would be widespread disagreement over beauty in obvious cases *within* a culture, but that borderline cases arise and the difficulties across cultures are almost insuperable. Japanese music to a Western ear is but one of a million examples. Beauty has some properties which are dependent on the culture from which they spring, but whatever the difficulties in classifying our thoughts it is no idle fancy that people should so often have thought of truth as being beauty. That truth is sometimes ugly is a reminder that the word "truth" can mean more than one thing.

"Simplicity is truth" could also be a beguiling idea. Certainly most of truth and most of our best ideas are simple. But note the catch; we call ideas "best" if they both work in *and* are also simple. Anyway, it is the simple ideas that we discover first and we are bound to have more of them than the complex ones, most of which are still to see the light of day. This is why cancer cannot yet be universally cured, because the disease and its relationship to the human being's internal organization are extremely complicated rather than conveniently simple.

Now let us fit the sections of the jigsaw of this chapter into one; the sky, the sea and the ship have been made in separate sections and we must now put them together.

The computer is a universal machine; it could be one of many but happens to be the only one so far developed on this scale. Its universality occurs because it is incomplete until it receives its program, and as a result we are able to choose a program which transforms it into anything we wish.

Now we come to our point about "machinelike operations". The point is that what is machinelike in a real sense of being automatic and involving no sort of insight can indeed certainly be dealt with by a computer. But this is not the limit of computing abilities. It is possible for computers to perform other sorts of operations which we sometimes call creative.

People in life make *ad hoc* decisions, they make rough guesses as to the best plan to adopt, they play games like chess by "rough-and-ready" rules of thumb. Such procedures are certainly not machinelike in the sense meant above. This is the reason why so many people have felt that to talk of machines thinking makes no sense. The answer to them is that machines in the wider sense of "what is capable of being constructed by artificial means" can perform these *ad hoc* decisions and use such planning methods.

In passing, we should mention another point of dimensions. Remember Jupiter is 483,000,000 miles from the sun, and living organisms have existed on the earth's surface for a hundred million years. In that state of mind, consider that a human nervous system is made up of about a hundred thousand million elements which we call "neurons". This has evolved over at least two million years to its present form, and in a more general form for nearer a hundred million years. Under these circumstances the extent to which in a mere thirty years we have come to build complex and highspeed systems, especially by programming computers, to behave so much like a human nervous system is most impressive. By the year 2000 or thereabouts we shall be at the same level of complexity of computer

C

system as the human nervous system and will have achieved such a goal in a mere 50 years, a fraction of a second as it were to achieve what has taken evolution a hundred million years. This is the measure of man's ability. His abstract skill and imagination are without equal, except in man's own imagination.

5 Cybernetics

"The idea of non-human devices of great power and great ability to carry through a policy, and of their dangers is nothing new. All that is new is that now we possess effective devices of this kind."

"Cybernetics"
Norbert Wiener

CYBERNETICS IS THE SCIENCE, above all others, that covers our main interests in this book. It is the science of communication and it is the science of control, and it deals precisely with the development both of the control of human behaviour and the manufacturing of artificial intelligence.

Cybernetics also involves the process of modelling human intelligence, and because such modelling is now made explicit it can be systematically improved, and since such systematic improvement is bound to be used by human beings to amplify their own intelligence, its crucial importance to society must be self-evident. We are gradually building a superspecies which is still part-man and part-machine; let us try to ensure we use it and use it efficiently rather than let it use us. The question of its proper use is in reality the central theme of the whole of this book.

Cybernetics is a subject with many different aspects. No single answer to the question of what the word 'cybernetics' means can satisfy everyone, partly because one can describe any subject at so many different levels of complexity. We can, as we have already said, describe electricity in one set of terms for the person who has just met electric light for the first time, in more complex terms for the electrician, and altogether differently for the quantum physicist. This matter we touched upon when considering what we mean by explanation. Apart from the degree of complexity involved, one can also place emphasis on the research side of the subject or on its application.

To make matters more complicated still, there are many different ways of defining terms, so if a definition is what is asked for then the problem is that much more difficult to deal with. There are dictionary makers' definitions which try to decide how words are used by most people, descriptive definitions which really explain what the word refers to, operational definitions, ostensive definitions (pointing) and many more besides. We shall start with some abstract statements about cybernetics and then try to make such statements more concrete.

Science in general we think of, as we have said, as being an attempt to answer specific questions in specific situations and for specific purposes. That this is sometimes tackled by setting up models and theories, whether they are formal, such as in a set of axioms, or not, does not alter the contextual nature of science. Perhaps indeed one can say more generally that theories and models in science are designed to answer questions of any degree of complexity.

Cybernetics has special reference to self-controlling or adaptive systems. Partly because of this, it does not draw an absolute distinction between the living and the non-living, since either living or non-living can be self-controlling and can be adaptive in behaviour.

Cybernetics attempts to provide a rigorous theory of adaptive systems of all sizes and kinds and of many different degrees of complexity. Its very breadth of application is the source of some misunderstanding, since it sometimes seems to claim the same status as the whole of science; this is not in fact the case, but its very breadth is one reason for our interest in it.

In practice, cybernetics cuts across the established sciences such as physics, chemistry and zoology by selecting those common features which contribute to a complete theory of communication and control. The adaptive feature suggests *negative feedback* as a vital factor, and while this reminds us of self-controlling machines at one level of complexity, it reminds us of human learning in the light of "knowledge of results" at another level.

The more mathematical features of cybernetics are embodied in fields known as theory of automata and theory of robots. This is because discussions of the foundations of the mathematics culminating, in part, in the work concerned with the structure of axiomatic systems—which are in effect theoretical machines—are very important to us. The relevancy of this work lies in the limitations which we now know apply to axiomatic systems. The mathematics mainly associated with cybernetics is that of *discrete* functions rather than *continuous* ones which is what classical mathematics has been mostly concerned with so far.

We should mention again that an axiomatic or axiom system is a set of statements, wherein some are the starting statements (axioms) and others are logically deduced from these. The best known example is Euclid's geometry, but a great deal of mathematics can be made axiomatic, as indeed can many other branches of knowledge.

The difficulty with axiom systems is that we need to have some external statements (outside the axiom system) which tell us whether the axiom system is, for example, consistent or not.

The other point of cybernetic interest is that if you have an axiom system that can be used to describe something then it can certainly be made in some sense into a machine. Unfortunately the opposite is not true: you can have a system which cannot be made into an axiom system, yet its function may still be performed by a machine.

The principal problem of cybernetics has been that of artificial intelligence. Can machines show some measure of intelligence, and if so to what extent can they do so? This we have already considered in some measure. Much of our mathematical theory tells us—since it supplies theoretical machines—what a particular machine would do without our actually having to build it. We can predict its behaviour from the blueprint alone.

The word 'machine', we must yet again remind the reader, as used by cyberneticians provides a special difficulty, particularly when featured in such issues as "Could machines be made to think?". We clearly do not mean 'machine' here to apply to those machinelike systems such as aeroplanes or motorbikes, which by the very definition of the word 'machinelike' are unthinking. We mean by 'machine' anything that is capable of being "made in the laboratory" and by man, at least "made by man" in the first instance, since machines can themselves make machines. There is a whole branch of cybernetics that deals with machines that make machines, as well as machines that service and repair themselves.

In such circumstances many people have construed cybernetics as being concerned with the artificial construction of human beings, whether by artificial seeds that are then made to grow into an embryo and human being, or directly. Either is presently quite outside our range of knowledge and our capabilities, but arguments still go on about such possibilities and their theoretical background. Neither are such discussions pointless, because the most important short-term reason for pursuing such apparently grandiose goals is not the later or ultimate achievement but the "fallout" which occurs en route, in the short term. Nevertheless there is little doubt that such major goals will themselves also be achieved.

The behavioural social and biological sciences are all directly related to cybernetics, in that they have many aspects which are concerned with control, communication, self-adaptation and evolution.

The primary desire to provide machinelike models of such complex systems as a human brain and a human nervous system has resulted in the production of models or partial systems which do some part of what the human brain can do. Pattern recognition is a vital basic thread that runs throughout these models, whether visual pattern recognition (the use of the eyes) or conceptual pattern recognition (thinking) as a basis for inductive logic. The difficulty lies in putting all these computer programs, as they usually are, together to provide a complete program of the individual; this will certainly come and will probably come before the end of the century.

The "bits and pieces" of the total cybernetic program have been systematically investigated and have told us more about concept and hypothesis formation, logic, language, decision-taking, problem-solving and thinking—both human and human-like. Here cybernetics overlaps psychology and logic, as well as semantics and mathematics, and recent progress has been very considerable.

As a result of these studies, we can now set up models, usually in the form of computer programs, that can perform some parts of these vital requirements listed above. These parts are gradually being combined so that the same program or set of programs can accept data, whether in ordinary English or otherwise, formulate concepts and hypotheses and test these concepts as people do in everyday life. This clearly is the beginning of a model of total human intelligence, and although in 1970 it still lacks human flexibility, provided it is geared into a sufficiently narrow sector of knowledge it has great advantages over the performance of the human being, and that applies even in the present. The advantages it possesses are above all those of speed and accuracy which reflect once more upon the extraordinary versatility of the computer.

It must be emphasized that the theory of cybernetics does not depend directly upon computers, and the hardware construction of cybernetic models can take the form of neuronlike structures made of chemicals or electronics, indeed can be any equipment at all which mirrors in some manner communication and control properties of adaptive systems, whether humanlike or utterly unhumanlike.

Cybernetics also obviously includes the study of "natural" control and communication systems such as are involved, for example, in the muscles of the body, the functioning of the internal bodily organs such as heart, lungs and liver, and the human nervous system and special senses such as eyes and ears in particular. The study of genetics is relevant to cybernetic "growth" models, as this is one of the ways in which we inherit the characteristics we do: Father's ugly nose and Grandma's ill-temper.

Cybernetics is directly relevant to society in general, simply because society and social systems in general are adaptive and depend essentially on control and communication. Systems and groups of people behave, in fact, very much like individuals.

It is clear that much of human learning stems from the social environment and if we wished to build a robot comparable to a human being it would have to exist in a social environment of some sort—presumably in a society of robots or a mixed society of human beings and robots. But in "down-to-earth" terms cybernetics is vital to a study of society, because it is also the science of management and the science of government. It adopts an attitude to business and commercial systems that is new: it treats them as adapting and evolving systems.

Discovering how the properties of adaptive systems operate helps us to understand how a business behaves, and how governments operate is very similar again and is very much part of our problems. The point is literally that a commercial firm or a government, or indeed any social group, is itself sufficiently like a human body for many of the same principles to apply to both; this is what cybernetics, like most of science, is mainly concerned with—resemblances among differences, as well as differences among resemblances.

At the level of practical applications it is the new type of computer programming that is most relevant to cybernetics. We all know that payroll, ledger-keeping, accounts, the use of statistical and mathematical methods and the like can be carried out on the computer. What is less well known is that "off-the-cuff" decisions and plans can also be so programmed. We have touched on this matter in both chapters 4 and 8, but will now treat it in more detail.

Consider the problem in general terms. If we are asked to hit upon the solution to a combination lock, we know, because the number of possible combinations are finite, that we can find the solution, but it may take months or even years. If we were asked to forecast exactly how many articles of a certain kind we would sell next month then we could not give a precise solution, except by guessing and hoping the guess was nearly correct. Both these sorts of cases call for special methods, since in the first case it is not economic to use the "precise" method of exhaustive search, and in the second case it is not possible because no "precise" method is, or can be, available.

The computer uses methods which are short cuts in the form of hypotheses, or models. They are adaptive so that when mistakes are made they are remedied for the next time, and the whole process is fast, *explicit* and makes the best possible use of all the available information, especially including the information fed back into it from previous results. This entails careful checking on the system being controlled, and results in the accumulation of experience. It is a bit like having a person who lives for ever and can accumulate experience for ever; he is bound, in the end, to become very knowledgeable and very intelligent.

Such special methods apply to a commander taking decisions in a war, or to a board of directors deciding, for example, whether to expand a section of the business, or to close up another section, to build a new factory or to shut up a particular part of an old factory, and so on and so forth.

Such special methods in numerical form are used for modelling the appropriate demand made on the business, providing estimates of sales, which is where a business starts.

It is possible as a result of the development of such short-cut techniques for the management of a company to make their decisions quickly and efficiently, and they can also steadily improve their standards.

There is also the use of the computer programmed to allow conversation in ordinary English, using typewriters rather than human voices, and this provides the possibility of quick and efficient data retrieval and inference-making. Over and above this, we can now see that any form of computation may be carried on inside the computer. This facility dovetails perfectly with the use of "short cuts" and with the process of explicitly learning by experience. When experience is not possible— where "one-off" decisions are called for—then simulation techniques are available. It should be added that since no existing computing store is large enough for us to provide a complete program for all of our purposes, this limitation applies also to the human being who stores the bulk of the information he uses in the environment, mainly in the form of books, journals and other people.

The main source of information, apart from the written word, to both human being and the computer must be "other people". The link with other people must necessarily—at least at the moment—be an ordinary language like English, and the type of information which forms the bulk of the computer store will be "reference" information. As usual, the short cut is that "What matters is not knowing things, but knowing where to find them"—either by data retrieval or by working by inference from first principles; much the same argument obviously applies to human education, as we pointed out at the time.

Finally, as far as society is concerned, it must be said that cybernetics really represents the quintessence of intelligent planning. Science is always the systematic application of that most uncommon quality misleadingly called "commonsense".

It should be noted that scientists use specialized terminology because they have to make distinctions at the level of detail sometimes demanded by science which we do not normally need to make in our ordinary lives. In particular, they often have to introduce precision of the kind associated with logic or engineering, and the business of making measurements, which along with precision one associates usually with mathematics.

It is the use of specialized techniques that is so vital to the business user. Everyone knows that computers are needed for their speed and accuracy, but not everyone knows that their potential has not yet been anything like fully realized. The field called operational research, which is really the application of scientific methods to anything and everything, supplies important models for prediction, but not everyone has seen the necessity for these plans to be dynamic and self-adapting.

Cybernetics provides a way of looking at things, a philosophy of systems, that is above all dynamic. By copying human beings and seeing where we can improve on them, we are gradually building a science of systems which applies to all social evolution, and which has special applications in business and government: that science is cybernetics.

We could fairly claim that the mathematical theory of information, systems theory, systems analysis, parts of market and motivational research and statistical theories of various kind are all a part of, or overlap, cybernetics. To those readers who are not interested in modern mathematics, let us simply say that these special methods help us to refine greatly the logic of our thinking and make it very much more precise.

A very general example of cybernetics applications should be given in this chapter, since it illustrates our problem quite well. If you had to decide between three or four different courses of action, how would you proceed? You might reasonably try to think out the consequences of each and weigh the probable outcomes against the cost. This applies whether you are deciding on where to invest money, what materials to use on constructing a bridge, or whether to cut down on armed forces in the interest of helping the country's financial state.

Regardless of the physical use to which the decision is to be put, the methods should not be *ad hoc* in the sense that most human beings make them so. There may be no specific methods for solution to the problem, but even the approximate methods used can be the subject of scientific investigation in a way which still makes them far better than human methods. Not to realize this is to believe that because all of mathematics cannot be made 'machinelike' in the narrow sense, it cannot be solved by a "machine". Granted you can apply some sort of measure to the cost of the undertaking and perhaps also to the risk of being wrong; you can establish some principle such as that of *minimum regret*, which tells you which will cause you least pain, or regret, if you are wrong.

A simple example is that of betting on horses. If you were asked to bet £1 or $3 at a horse race meeting, you would not bother too much how you placed the bet and you would probably follow the optimist's strategy and take a chance; this probably means putting it all on an outsider you fancy. But if you are told to bet £10 or $30 of your own money, you are likely to be more cautious, since you will regret the loss of such an amount. If it becomes £100 or $300 or, even worse, £1,000 or $3,000, then your whole attitude will change. You will start hedging your bets, and generally considering how to cut your possible losses; you are now really minimizing your regret.

Another feature of such decision-taking, or decision-processing as it is sometimes called, is the compromise between ends and means.

If you want a really good meal you will not necessarily insist on flying to Paris to get it, but will settle for one only slightly less attractive right here in London or New York. In other words you do not fix ends first and then fix means, you juggle the two together.

In the last example, you have two probabilities to consider. One refers to the probable standard of the meal and the other to the probability of ease of getting to the restaurant. To this double probability you can, of course, under considerations of urgency or vital importance of outcome, still apply your principle of minimum regret.

Procedures which are of the "fail safe" variety and the systemizing of risk are intuitively understood, but no human can match the computer model when the situation over which the decision is taken is complicated. The human being does not generally try to deal with complexity, he usually ignores it.

Psychological features of the environment suggest that, after precise information processing has been carried out, it is still the individual's "hunch" that really matters in decision-taking. We can agree with this in part but not to the exclusion of carrying out the precise part of the process through the cybernetic model and probably working it out on the computer. Furthermore, this distinction will not always be valid since increasingly cyberneticians are building the situation's psychological factors into the models used. This is again a typical part of the development of cybernetics.

One aspect of cybernetics we should mention is that of emotions and the complete man. Later in the book, in chapter 11, we discuss the emotional world, but here it is important to pave the way for this discussion by looking at the whole matter from a cybernetic point of view.

We can think of our problem this way. Cybernetics, or certainly some cyberneticians, claim that there is nothing a human being can do that an artificial system could not be made to do. We have seen the manner in which this issue is pursued in the case of rational thinking, logic and the use of language. But are we also asserting that machines like computers will in the future be able to paint, write poetry and feel the emotions of love and hate, friendship and all the things that typify human behaviour? If this is being claimed we must learn a little about how it might be done.

First of all, in terms of artificially intelligent computer programs for existing computers, we could only copy such emotions by trying to see how they would affect our judgements over rational matters. This highlights our problem. The role of the emotions is like a fuse-box. They make it easier to run away or get angry, and they produce a short-circuited early warning system.

In evolution, without emotions we, as human beings, could not have survived. As we establish our survival by becoming social and inventive, living in groups and constructing buildings and weapons, so the role of emotions is extended. While still acting as a fuse-box warning system, they become associated with the signs and symbols of our language and logic. We associate a red face with anger or tiredness, a white face with fear, just as we associate dark clouds with rain.

If we are to actually reproduce such a system, it must, in all probability, be constructed organically. We need organic materials such as human flesh and bones and this is not yet possible. Plastics will provide our answer. We could even manufacture "seeds" which grow under the control of a master program into what we might call biological computers.

Why should we build such things? Partly to increase our understanding of how human beings behave, but partly, and this is more sinister, to use in autonomous robots in order to try to control them.

The "crunch" is not about music, poetry or painting, since these are by-products of the mixture of emotions, reason and imagination in humans, but about control. You cannot change the opinion of a non-emotional system except by changing his goals; you can never appeal to his social feelings, since he has none. The only way we can have a tolerable world for human beings to live in is to make emotional appeals possible. We cannot abide a "legalistic" life and cannot live in such a narrow rational or mechanical world.

In other words, love and affection are vital ingredients for living, and these are vital as the result of social life superimposed upon our instinctive behaviour patterns and our emotions.

Cyberneticians will certainly want to claim that they can reproduce such biological systems artificially, and the main requirement is a far more detailed knowledge of chemistry and biochemistry.

We could in the end finish up by making a human being in the laboratory. Some people might think this futile. But when we can do such a thing, and it will be many years in the future before we do, we shall have unlocked many of the major secrets of chemistry and biology.

We are assuming that the arts, as viewed from the point of view of cybernetics, can and would emerge from an artificial species. But just as Japanese music is very different from Western music, so we would expect our new species' art to be different from our own. We are certainly showing our hand now. There is nothing we feel that will not be changed by cybernetics.

Indeed like most subjects—but even more so—the confines of cybernetics are large and not precisely defined, and although they may be definable, such precision is wholly undesirable at the moment. If you have a system—whether a mechanical toy, a business, a string of retail shops, a defence radar network or a human being—provided it is adaptive and capable of accumulating knowledge, in simple or complex ways, then its study is central to cybernetics, and cybernetics is the central science of the second industrial revolution which is the primary subject of this book.

6 The Automated Society

"What they are really observing, however, is the automation of human limitations, we are enshrining in steel, glass and semi-conductors, the very limitations of hand, eye and brain which the computer was invented precisely to transcend."

"Decision and Control"
Stafford Beer

"The Task of Industry:
1. A greater ability to translate new ideas into practical reality."
"The Automatic Factory—Dream or Nightmare"
Sir Walter Puckey

AUTOMATION is applied cybernetics. This is perhaps not historically correct, since automation really came first in the form of self-controlling factories, and in the engineering of automatic control systems. But now that theory has caught up with and even passed practice, we can think of automation as being the application of cybernetic ideas.

'Automation' is a word that tends to make people emotional. It makes them strike postures because it is a subject much misunderstood and therefore a source of some fear.

We have heard the word 'automation' used a great deal, especially in the last decade, but not many of the facts surrounding it nor much of its significance for society have really been made clear; the reasons for this are unfortunate, but *are* quite clear.

The scientific world is a specialist world, and made up mostly of specialists who will not—as a matter of doctrine—explain their purposes, nor will they explain the far-reaching consequences of their discoveries and inventions. This is because they themselves do not appreciate the wider context in which their ideas will be used and the changes they will bring about. Furthermore, there is an unwritten but clear rule that scientists should not speculate and prognosticate about the future. Their job, as they so often say, is to find things out and leave the application to others. It is the opposite of the old service dictum. It is "You are paid to think and not to do anything, or even talk about your ideas".

All this is tragically wrong, and the scientist must be encouraged even to exaggerate the possibilities of the future in order to awaken the awareness of the peoples of the world to what is happening to them. It is not widely realized that university politics too are often narrow and vicious, but this we shall be explaining in a later chapter.

Automation is concerned with the automatic control of machinery. Once upon a time, men and women did all the control jobs such as stamping forms, cashing cheques, issuing the payroll, writing up the ledger, and so on and so forth. Now it can be done and is being done by machines, and mostly by that rather special machine, the computer. Almost everyone is aware that the age of the quill pen has passed, although unaware of what has taken its place, or of the implications of its passing.

First of all we must say that such effects are cumulative and work in a highly accelerated way. They gather ground so quickly that before we are aware of it our society has changed, and perhaps for the worse.

Consider for a moment a well-known and early example of automation—the automatic pilot GEORGE. Many human pilots have used it and most people have heard of it. But how does it work?

The principles involved are exceptionally simple. An aircraft is controlled as to its direction of flight by its rudder, elevators and ailerons. We set the desired positions for each and then if they are displaced from the desired position record the fact, thus changing the direction of flight. The human pilot registers the fact visually by watching his instruments and, where possible, by seeing the aircraft has changed its position with respect to the horizon. All we need, in order to replace the pilot for the purpose of keeping the aircraft on course, is a sensitive element that records the error in position and immediately provides the equivalent compensation on the control. It is like driving a car; if you see that you are too far to the left you rotate your steering wheel to the right.

To build such a device provided quite a problem for engineers, but they did it. They began then to realize that the principle of control through *negative feedback*—this is the process of being provided with the information which makes you correct any error—is a very powerful one and applies to hosts of different systems such as the operation of the human brain and other internal body organs. To maintain purposes and achieve goals, you must know the results of your action.

GEORGE, the automatic pilot, was used to keep a steady direction and steady speed of flight. Bumpiness in the air made control movements necessary and these control movements could be made *automatically*. But the human pilot was still there to "keep an eye on things" and to be sure all went well. GEORGE was never intended to be a substitute pilot, but could do a part of the pilot's job very well indeed.

This is how the public at large think of automation: clever devices which can save human labour, provided always the whole thing is ultimately under human control.

The argument about the social effects of automation has been simple enough. The economic facts of life limit the extent to which we can build motorways and freeways, however desirable they may be; similarly, the progress of automatic controls will be slow. We shall replace the least skilled of human beings first, since the simplest operations are the easiest to automate.

All of this is only a tiny fraction of the total consequences of automation. So far we have seen only a little fear expressed: an increasing amount of standardization, but little difference in the attitudes of trade unionists or employers, even as we begin to see the rise in the cost of personal services.

Here is the core of the matter: men are even more costly than machines, and as a result machines are used more and more. This is particularly the case as they become more and more efficient. Nor will their cost go up, since machines can manufacture themselves. Most commentators on automation tacitly assume that machine costs will rise proportionately to human labour costs since human beings are needed to make machines. But this is false. The most urgently needed machines are those for making machines, where *both* machines—those that do the making *and* those that are made—are automatic and self-controlling. This is one of the ways in which cybernetics has changed altogether our picture of the future automated society.

We know that machines can reproduce themselves as well as repair and maintain themselves. This does not mean that over-night the influx of such machines to transform our society will appear; if such a thing did happen it would lead to a world crisis, and immediate destruction of the human race. But it does mean the gradual emergence of such machines which taken together with cybernetic machines imply the emergence of our new dominating species.

It is worth reflecting for a moment on the degree of control we as human beings are likely to be able to exercise on machines as they become increasingly sophisticated. We find it easy enough to control the complicated but docile machines like a lawn mower, although cars and aircraft provide certain problems. Simple "feedback" systems are a bit more difficult, but we can always switch off the power supply, and we should ask ourselves under what conditions we could no longer switch off the power supply of our "more intelligent machines".

The best way of answering this last question is to take a more or less realistic example of a possible use of automation. Suppose we decide to build individual machines to wage a war for us. We need to make them highly flexible since they are *not* going to have a human controller, and without great flexibility they would be an easy prey to an enemy. What we have to do is build a great deal of humanlike intelligence into the machine, and it is worth thinking carefully how this should be done; we are, in effect, building a robot soldier.

We can build artificial ears and eyes—radio sets and televisions are the simplest artificial analogy—and we can build a large store to collect information. This store is essentially a computer which can reason for itself if appropriately motivated, and here we have the key to the situation. Intelligent behaviour requires motivation; it must have purposes or goals.

We must bear in mind that in building intelligent machines

we are directly copying human beings. The only reason that we know we want to get to London is because we want to get to the theatre which is in London, and then we try to find out why we want to go to the theatre. A whole trail of motivations leads us back to the ultimate goal of survival. Events which are satisfying and good for survival become associated with other events, which as a result become goals in themselves. It is the job of motivational research to unravel all these chains, some of which are typical of all people and some of which vary from individual to individual. If you dislike the name 'Judith' the reason is because you have experienced some association with that name which is unpleasant; the difficulty often lies in tracing the association. Mostly we do not even try to do so, we just like or dislike things without knowing why.

To decide on a course of action and carry it through requires a clearcut goal, and the measure of success of the action is the extent to which the goal is achieved. By this means a human being or an "intelligent" machine can modify the behaviour needed. We achieve the flexibility which characterizes human behaviour and this is partly done by the dangerous business of associations with success or failure, likes and dislikes.

We need such flexibility in our autonomous "machine soldier" and there can be no guarantee that "he" with his newly designed independence, so necessary for his job, will not be turned against his makers.

The situation is absurd, yet quite real. One sees perhaps a glimmer of hope from the way we have controlled actual human beings in the past. After all, they have not always rebelled against authority and turned on their makers. But here there are problems, since human beings have a conscience and have emotions which are dragooned by early training, as we have already mentioned.

Music, poetry and religion all work towards harmony and provide a sense of satisfaction in humans which compensates for much of the drudgery they have to suffer. The snag is that our machine will have no such emotions, unless we take the risk of including them. It will anyway be motivated to eliminate an enemy, but will also have the flexibility and "intelligence" to modify motivations through experience. We have to be sure that the modifications enacted will not lead to an elimination of ourselves. Such an assurance cannot be forthcoming beyond a certain level of intelligence in the machine; and this is the way that we could therefore make a new species which is more efficient than we are ourselves.

We would not give this species the power to reproduce itself, but if we give it the intelligence and the ability to learn, it will discover for itself how to reproduce itself. This is one of the central themes of a consideration of the future of automation and cybernetics and one we shall return to again and again.

We must now go back to the present. Here we find the emergence of automatic trains, monorails, driverless cars and pilotless aircraft. These are immediate possibilities and visitors to Expo 67 at Montreal will have seen the first two in action.

The only barrier to this easy and immediate type of auto-mation is the sheer expense of application. There are still tech-nical difficulties to overcome, but these are relatively minor and provided the money is available the work can certainly be done. The direction taken is precisely that which leads to the problem of the autonomy of intelligent machines. It is even suggested that this is precisely the same problem as that of giving man "free will". The comparison stands irrespective of whether the "free will" is a gift from God or something that has emerged in evolution as a result of the growth of human intelligence.

The first and most obvious of automated developments is the automated "local" aircraft. We have at the moment small aircraft which fly from airport to airport after careful flight plan arrange-ments have been made. This facility is only available to a few people who are either wealthy or flying enthusiasts or both. The development of automated equipment, already partly developed for intermissile interception, will allow small aircraft to avoid each other in the way that birds do; they can be com-pletely programmed for specific flights. The idea of a froglike jumping aircraft, with additional flying capacity, will lead to the development of the equivalent of private cars.

Cars themselves can be automatically controlled and, as a result, release the driver to carry out other activities while he is being conveyed from place to place. These will be local journeys since for longer journeys monorail and aircraft are inevitable, with or without car ferry facilities.

Our social system will clearly be wholly automated and nowhere more obviously so than in the home itself. Consider the kitchen. We can automate this quite easily.

First of all think of cooking. The input is the raw material, the groceries we buy, and the meats and poultry, bread, milk, etc., that we keep in the larder. Much of this can be circulated by other means than are even used effectively by the present supermarket methods, but we shall not at the moment concentrate on this aspect of the problem but assume that the raw materials are needed and available. We assume we have our input and the cooked meal as output from the kitchen, and this clearly makes the kitchen a subsystem of the total system of the household. As soon as we think of automating the kitchen so that the cooker is under thermostatic control and food is placed in it and taken out of it automatically rather than by hand, it is clear that our familiar problem of "rethinking a problem" is absolutely vital.

We cannot do things the old way now, so we change our methods to fit the new way. We shall have, perhaps, a two-doored cooker with doors opening to allow a conveyor belt to provide the input and then opening again to allow the same belt to provide the output, the belt containing, of course, whatever dishes, etc., that are needed to contain items to be cooked. It could even be a one-doored cooker with a reversing mechanism; the future for equipment designers would seem unlimited.

The same conveyor belt system leads out of the kitchen and into the room where eating takes place; this is almost certainly in the next room. There would be another input belt which goes through a similar sort of box to the oven where dishwashing takes place. Indeed, the box is probably more sophisticated than just an input–output oven and is probably a place where dishes are stacked and washing takes place under fairly complicated conditions of soap and water supply. It seems certain that the best place to keep the dishes stored is the place where they are washed. After they are washed, they are brought out only when they have to be used for the next meal. However, regardless of the details of the organization, it is clear that a certain measure of rethinking is necessary. In some areas all cooking for the community will be centralized in a simple building and your input to the kitchen will be already cooked. This implies a community type of life, familiar in some forms of fascism and communism which are a prototype for the future. This goes against the grain for most people, but we know how quickly and efficiently we can adapt, or be brainwashed.

The rethinking of the kitchen also involves the rethinking of the storage of utensils and oddments which are necessary for the total meal. For example, the idea of a larder where the housewife keeps breakfast cereals, mayonnaise and the like must go; we must substitute a system whereby all the necessary ingredients for a meal whether involved in cooking or the washing-up process must be on the conveyor belt system. The field of sauces, mayonnaise and the like must be kept at hand in a cupboard near to the place where eating actually takes place; in fact, of course, not in the kitchen at all but in the dining room, unless of course these two rooms become one. We could carry on this story of domestic bliss into greater and greater detail, but the main points are too obvious to mention.

The housewife under these automated conditions must surely be in a condition of controlling a console, like a radio set or television, which will normally be in the dining room, just outside the conveyor belt hatch leading to and from the kitchen, and the various buttons which she can press will simply dictate to the computer what is to be cooked and how.

It is easy to see how the domestic arrangements of traditional household kitchens could be resolved in this automated way, provided the proper organization and ordering goes on. A particular meal is ordered by appropriate button-pressing on the console; provided also sufficient time is given to achieve the ends, the meal will be planned by the computer, cooked— where necessary—and served on to the table by the conveyor belt controlled by the computer. The only human problem is its consumption. This itself is a further reminder of the overhanging fear of boredom, since many people like cooking, and for many it has been the "means" in life that have served as ends.

The very fact of a conveyor belt producing meals on plates suggests that the dining table of the future—unless tradition dies too hard—should be that one should eat on either side of the conveyor belt which should itself perform the role of the table. Much here depends on whether one wishes to add more to the purely utilitarian aspects of the automated process or not. There are psychological and social reasons for believing that the purely utilitarian will never wholly hold sway. Individuality must express itself, and here is just such a chance.

Dishwashing activities could, of course, be cut out altogether; we could have throwaway utensils and even throwaway dishes, and this would involve a problem of dumping wastage. Wastage is in any case involved, and it is taken for granted that a suitable garbage disposal unit will be available in the future.

The next phase which may well have been reached by 2000 is that of taking one's food by pill. But psychological needs rather than nutritional needs will still provide at least one meal per day. The alternative, as we have mentioned, lies in the communal model of life.

We have mentioned the process of "rethinking" more than once; this is a very vital process in many phases of life and it is important to grasp the principle clearly. We have already mentioned GEORGE, the automatic pilot, but let us now look again at this type of automatic control from the viewpoint of rethinking. In building the automatic control systems we would be stupid to try to manufacture artificial eyes to read the various dials showing height, airspeed and the like that are currently standard input equipment in an aircraft cockpit. The point here is that visual displays in the form of dials are purely for human eyes. If we do not have human controls we do not *need* visual displays. This means that the automatic pilot of tomorrow can receive details of airspeed communicated directly into its control system. Because of such rethinking, huge simplications can be achieved. Indeed, the alternative would be to ignore rethinking and produce the ludicrous and ponderous robots of early science fiction. Wheels are more convenient than legs for locomotion; the only snag is that we build houses with stairs for human legs and to use these we should need some artificial leg systems.

Before we leave altogether our example of the "domestic bliss" presented by automation, let it be emphasized that it was only illustrative in a narrow context of the private house today.

In the future we shall change our community life and move away from isolated private houses to something more like interrelated networks of motels; this suggests community life with a difference. In turn it suggests the emergence of new linear cities that are built around motorways, stretching across whole continents.

The first Industrial Revolution was based directly upon the development of the steam engine. Here was a really large power amplifier, which replaced man's muscular power. Previous to this big step in power amplification, wheels, levers and other more primitive gadgets and instruments had already made it abundantly clear that man could and would use his ingenuity in the fight to gain control of his environment.

The discovery of electricity and the gradual realization of its full potential combined with the emergence of the steam engine to produce the revolution. These, with other engineering inventions, led directly to the Industrial Revolution with all its wealth and all its squalor. The squalor occurred through lack of planning and control, the wealth came from applied science and technology. A good example of one development outstripping another.

The two main causes of confusion over the next phase of development of automation are partly due to a failure to distinguish mechanization from automation. Since this distinction is in any case a matter of degree, some confusion is understandable. Mechanization is the amplification of muscular power, while automation is the amplification of brain power.

Intelligence, in fact, is a matter of degree since it is possible to have automatic control at any level of complexity. The automatic temperature control as set by a human is one thing but the human's method for making the setting is another. This machine of the second level is itself contingent upon further features of the environment, and so it can continue to higher levels of intelligence. Machines of higher orders become more and more dependent on more and more remote factors in their environment, which introduces once more the motivations and purposes which determine human intelligence.

There are difficulties involved in scrutinizing the process of living in society as the very act of scrutiny is itself a part of living in that society; we cannot, as we have said before, "stop the world and get off". We can never get wholly outside ourselves, either as individuals or as groups. We are never privileged observers, outside the system of things, so all we do must be done implicitly. This principle of implicitness applies everywhere. If we wish to reconstruct or reorganize a factory and change our form of production, or if we wish to incorporate new designs into various arts and crafts, such as architecture or town planning, or in the building of new highways, then we have to face the difficulty of changeover, the transition from one state to another.

We are always in a state of transition, and still we have not become fully aware that transitions are our *normal* process of evolution, not by any means the abnormal times that they are sometimes thought to be. This is another way of saying that society has been slow to recognize the vitally important nature of change, and this we have already extensively emphasized.

Cybernation and automation have brought many of these things into focus. The word 'automation' applies to both the process of automatic operating and to the more general problem of making things automatic. It is concerned with the development of machinery which is capable of different degrees of automatic control. It is an application of cybernetics, which in turn is defined as the science of communication and control, and is especially concerned with artificial intelligence.

There are many jokes about computerized systems going wrong; there are even more jokes about human beings going wrong, or being wholly inept, or—and this does not apply to computers and automated systems in general—being too lazy to do what is required of them. Here we are omitting altogether discussion of the tragic fate of the psychotic; no machine yet comes into this category.

The jokes about computer systems and automated systems usually involve their failure to show insight, so that they are capable of quite blithely sending every single copy of a whole issue of a journal to one single contributor. This is not, of course, a criticism of the program, but of the programmer who has not catered sufficiently for possible major errors. Nor is it a criticism of machines in that they cannot have the necessary flexibility and insight. The criticism is in reality that insight should perhaps be available for carrying out even simple automatic processes.

The above situation calls for comment on various scores, one at least being that human beings mostly are not used efficiently by the community. The bulk of jobs are automatic and require no insight and the result is boredom.

Should our educational system do what we ask of it, we shall have better and better educated people in our community. If such people are not released from dull routine jobs, we simply sow the seeds of discontent, rising to the point of violence and revolution.

Such an argument is sound, but in the end it is clear that failure to employ automated systems implies the total failure of the society in which we live. This is not so just because if we do not do it others will, but because if we do not follow the evolution of knowledge then civilization ceases to be motivated by natural curiosity and natural powers of experimentation. It is, in fact, inconceivable that this could occur.

There is no suggestion that people will be any happier living in the automated world of the twenty-first century. Happiness is something to do with the ratio of ambition to achievement as well as one's physiological state, and has nothing to do with material standards of the time, unless one is significantly below the average, and this is anyway catered for by the ratio of ambition to achievement. People are happy when they are physically fit and physiologically efficient, provided they have a fair measure of success in life—judged by their own standards—and no obvious weakness which they let become an obsession.

If a person feels he is missing some vital feature in life—such as satisfactory intercourse—then he becomes obsessed with the need, and as a direct result goes some way to ensure continued failure. This is like the psychology of rationing, whereby an item that is rationed has its demand greatly increased, an article whose price is doubled has greater demand, a woman covered by clothes is more desirable and the source of greater need than one who is naked. This only applies in each case provided a certain minimum intrinsic standard has been achieved by the commodity in question.

All of this makes clear why automation is a necessity and like all necessities a negative one. In the having of it we are little better off; without it, and with knowledge of what we are missing, we are bitterly unhappy.

It is the adaptive capacity of man that has so far made nonsense of all absolute standards.

At this stage of the book we have reached a turning point. We are moving away from the science of science, in order to see what effect such a fast developing science is having on our main institutions. Since we are also looking for solutions to our ever-increasing problems which are being created by science itself, we look first at education.

7 Education

"It took more than one million years to reach the present level (of civilization); it could double in the next thirty years."

Roger Revelle
Science Journal, 1967

"Accuse not Nature, she hath done her part;
Do thee but thine."

"Paradise Lost", Book viii
Milton

IN THE NEXT chapter we shall consider the academic world: the world of ideas, of research and of some teaching. Education will clearly be involved, but sometimes, indeed all too often, it is involved as a minor theme. Certainly university interest is primarily in the almost "private" research niche supplied by academic life, and the role that it plays in generating ideas in Western society.

In this chapter we are going to look at education at all levels and for all ages and for all people; education here is quite vital, and is concerned with the widest possible issues. We are looking to see what it has achieved, what it could achieve as well as what it should and must achieve if civilization is to have any hope of survival; education must be our main hope. Not that the survival of civilization depends upon education alone, for it does not, but without the necessary and urgently needed new educational system, whatever chances we have are greatly diminished, and become perhaps negligible.

Most people will agree that even from a short-term viewpoint in their discussions of Utopia, or at least in their desire to make a better world to live in, the arguments and the plans, as well as the hopes, return to education again and again.

Much of education today is a great deal better than it was even in the 1930s. Public schools in Britain are more civilized, and state schools are far better equipped. In America, education is more flexible than it was, and many experiments in education are occurring on both sides of the Atlantic.

In spite of the fact that we are improving, there must be grounds for doubting that we are improving sufficiently quickly. Do we really understand what we are trying to achieve and why, and do we really see the full scope of education and why it so urgently needs to be developed?

The fact that UNESCO some few years ago chose "Education for Leisure" as the theme of the year suggests at least that there is some awareness that education is not something that should only occur between the ages of six and sixteen.

When the word 'education' is used in casual conversation, most people conjure up a picture of classrooms, blackboards, chalk and an air of austerity. The figure of the master or mistress which accompanies this semi-memory of school life was once dressed in a mortar board and gown, accompanied even by swishing sticks which suggested that the desire to learn is not always innate in the young.

Education as a concept is appealed to again and again as the source of lack of understanding, and the inability to change. "We cannot rehouse that group of people because they will put their coal in the bath, at least they would if they had a bath." Getting the horse before the cart is the most important thing in the world and it is not easy to do because the cart-and-horse image is too simple; in practice so many activities are inter-related, so that each feature has to be treated in parallel with the others.

We cannot stop the clock and take "time out" to investigate things and come back to start the whole process on a new basis another day. We are having to remodel the system from within and this is never easy. It was once said of philosophy that it was like rebuilding a ship plank by plank while the ship was at sea; exactly the same applies to education, and indeed to each and every aspect of our society.

Let us first take up the almost traditional view of education, that it is something that begins at six and ends at sixteen and prepares you for life by teaching you basic skills in order to qualify you for a job, while some moral precepts are also thrown in to make you an acceptable member of society. Our education system has improved greatly in the last century, but in many ways most scholastic education is still of the nineteenth, and much of it of the eighteenth, century.

Education applies, of course, to more than schools, and within schools education should be much more than the mere efficient transmission of information from person to person. Nevertheless, this vital role of communicating information has to be performed, and we should ask carefully what progress it has made so far and what it must do in the future. The very word 'communication' reminds us of the relation of education to cybernetics.

School for most children is a fixed organization that, in its role of information processor, is inefficient, even a source of unhappiness sometimes bordering on misery. The unhappiness springs from two sources. The first source is that western society has social goals which are deeply embedded in cocktails, sex and sport, which provide the associations and the routes to the main goals of social and financial success. Secondly, there exists a teaching staff which is only half aware of the need for transmitting information about literature, religion, science and the like. All the time, those concerned have a nagging doubt as to whether all this matters or not.

One understands and sympathizes with the dilemma in which schools are placed by the parents, by the existing climate of social opinion and by the universities. Schools are really off-shoots of universities. This is so in the sense that schools are set goals such as O-level and A-level in Britain and high school graduation in America. These are necessary stages by which the youngsters step up to the universities. The universities set the examinations and the standards and, on the whole, make the schools conform to their needs and wishes. It should be re-membered that the selection process is such that schoolteachers, like university teachers, are seldom worldly people and most often are those whose only experience of the outside world (outside school) is university, so it is understandable that university is, by and large, the goal they impose on their students.

Schools in Britain are geared to university entrance. The teachers' difficulty is that they know this may not be an appropriate goal for even the majority of their students.

Let us ask ourselves how the task of transmitting information is achieved. Most schools have a rigid timetable which requires that their pupils, upon the ringing of a bell, think Latin for an hour, then upon the ringing of another bell, think French or mathematics for a further hour, and so on. We are now on ground that will be familiar to many people. But before running head-on into a discussion of the recipes for change, let us step back from the detailed scene and remind ourselves of the primary purposes of education. We have here many opinions to draw on and we choose John Stuart Mill's opinion; what follows is his notion of education. He said of education that it is:

> "The culture which each generation purposely gives to those who are to be its successors, in order to qualify them for at least keeping up, and if possible for raising, the level of improvement which has been attained."

This is the minimum requirement that needs to be satisfied by any educational system. But the problem has been that we have at best been satisfied with minimum requirements and at worst with almost irrelevant ones; all this is a little reminiscent of evolution, with its minimum requirement for survival.

It is quite vital that educational methods should be revised in the future in the light of modern scientific information. In particular, attention must be paid to psychological matters, to logic and to language. Indeed, it should be obvious that all aspects of science are in some way related to what is in essence another problem of good communication; it is in fact the most important example of communication that we meet in the whole of our lives.

Education may be thought of as being based on simple instinctive responses which were inherited directly from generation to generation in almost all species. What marks off the human being from other species is not only the more varied and complex learning that is built up around our instinctive behaviour patterns, but above all the ability to describe information in some sort of language.

Education, in the broad sense, is a process of development which results from specific communication as well as exposure to appropriate environments of all kinds. It is also necessary for people to have active participation in that environment. This is an essential condition for an educational system to be effective at all.

Education is a development primarily of knowledge *by description*, but with vital ingredients of knowledge *by acquaintance*.

Knowledge by description is open to human beings only, for all practical purposes, since only human beings use language and accumulate knowledge by handing it on through the medium of language.

In teaching, in the narrow sense of communicating information, we teach most of geography and history, for example, by description. This is obviously due to financial reasons in the main, since we cannot send children all over the world to actually see all the countries and all the types of vegetation and climate. But in the case of history, we have not yet got to the point where we can send people back through time. There is, though, another point to be made here and that is that you could not learn all of geography by direct acquaintance anyway, since it is also concerned with maps and charts, which are rather like types of pictures; this is very much an example of knowledge by description.

The great value of knowledge by acquaintance comes out in teaching the experimental or domestic skills, like woodwork and sewing. Everyone believes that direct acquaintance with the apparatus in a scientific experiment is quite necessary.

In the broader context of education, we see acquaintance as operating where children should see their teachers and parents themselves practising the moral codes they pretend to believe in. All too often, of course, this is not exactly what takes place.

Although education in schools is our primary concern in this chapter, this cannot, as we have said, be wholly separated from education in universities. This in turn is impossible to separate from adult life. This means that we must have the whole picture in mind all the time; we are forced to consider the needs of the whole course of the child's future life, and this applies to his emotional and social needs as well as to the purely academic.

This makes great demands on any system which cannot always be met in practice but can at least be met in the best possible way wherever there is sufficient flexibility to give maximum consideration to the child's individual needs.

It is clear that modern science has had an influence on education, even in 1970, but it is also clear that its influence has been altogether too slow in making itself felt. A. C. D. Peterson, the well-known educationalist, has said:

> "The great reforms in education which we have seen in the last hundred years of western civilization have undoubtedly come from the transference of our attention away from the teacher and the material taught to the child or adolescent and the process of learning."

This is one of many recent reminders that our increased knowledge of the learning process, and the ideal circumstances in which people absorb and utilize information, has certainly placed emphasis on the receiver of the information; the pupil has been concentrated on at the expense of the teacher. The teacher in the past had been greatly overemphasized in education, and therefore it is perhaps just that part of the balance should be redressed, even at the risk of overtipping the scales in the opposite direction.

Again we quote A. C. D. Peterson:

> "Teaching still plays a part in most learning and within the period of formal education professional teachers have a role to play."

What then is the proper nature of that role? This is an area of education which, in our recent justified concentration on the pupil's role, has been neglected.

This neglect of the teacher may have held up a beneficial reconsideration of our educational system. The teacher of tomorrow is going to become the individual tutor; and this represents a fundamental change of role. At the same time he will be required to show flexibility and organizational skill.

The school system, and education generally, is in the process of being automated. But unlike the factory, where the fewer people we see the better we are pleased, this does not apply to the school. Schools are for training human beings and as in the case of the university the essential part of this training is to make

D

them human. Human beings are essential to the process and there will be many more human beings available for the purpose in the future, where the bulk of teachers will be on a part-time basis and be able to concentrate far more attention on the individual needs of the children.

Let us look again at the narrower communication process that is basic to education.

We start from the observation that classroom teaching is inadequate. The main reason for this is that in a class of children of very different abilities and interests the teacher is forced to aim at teaching the average student. He has to assume a level of knowledge and hope to make a sort of average rate of progress. He therefore teaches inappropriately by being either too fast or too slow for a large minority, possibly even a majority, of the class. From this point of view, a method like the Dalton plan, in which each child progresses through a school at his own pace and the conventional classroom system is abolished, would be far more efficient. This means that he does most of his work alone or in small groups, with only occasional lectures and practically no classroom teaching in the traditional sense.

The disadvantage of the Dalton plan in the past has been that it has involved too much written work and too few teachers. Teachers have found themselves overworked, especially in correcting this written work. This is itself righted by an increase in the number of teaching staff.

Much more immediately important though is the advent of programmed instruction and teaching machines. The Dalton plan can, as a result, be put into operation with much less written work, and consequently correcting of this work, as well as much less supervision from the teacher. This is because programmed books, and often programmed information now under computer control, take away the need for writing merely to show that knowledge has been attained.

We are thinking of programmed instruction throughout as a process of question-and-answer, where the student may make up his own answer or select one of a number of answers to questions which he has been asked. The questions are based on texts which occur either on the screen of a computer output terminal, a teaching machine or book. Programmed instruction is a characteristically cybernetic type of system. It is self-teaching by use of preprepared texts, with the supplied answer completing the "feedback loop". It is clear that this must go hand-in-hand with closed circuit television, film loops, radio and television programmes, and indeed with every sort of audio-visual teaching aid.

In discussing cybernetics in chapter 5, we talked of the use of computers for solving *ad hoc* problems and making "off-the-cuff" decisions. This very technique applies now, not only to the organization of the material to be learned by the children and students generally, but also the organization of the school as a whole. Without such "heuristic" methods as they are often called, such problems will be too difficult to handle.

The use of the computer for *ad hoc* or heuristic methods directly stems from copying the methods of the best human decision-takers and planners, but now we have made the methods explicit, so they can be improved upon and handed on, by description, from generation to generation.

The dual approach is to use programmed instruction and other audio-visual aids in the context of the Dalton plan. This will be the basis of all school organization by the turn of the century. Such an approach allows us to concentrate on the human side of education, knowing all the time that the factual needs of the child are being catered for. This is so because with programmed instruction the speed of learning is greatly increased; therefore, if we use such a method to cover the basic material of most courses, much more time will be left both for the teacher and for the pupil to spend on the more interesting, individual, and in many ways more important, side of education. This involves a wider understanding of knowledge, science, religion, etc., and especially education in sex and social matters.

The plan is that, after a certain age, instead of having conventional timetables, schedules are drawn up stating what each child should know at a given period of his education. This could be done, for example, in periods of half-terms, and the schedules would act as goals, or subgoals, for the children. Teaching programmes will be written—many exist now in 1970—which will enable the child to cover this basic course material well within the specified time, with each child proceeding at his own rate.

The best arrangement will be for children to take the programmes supervised by a teacher to help them with particular
difficulties they might encounter. Here the teacher has become
the tutor. As each child finishes the course, he is given independent work to do. In this way, the material in the basic
syllabus is made interesting and given point, and the child is
encouraged to use his own initiative and to develop a certain
critical independence, something desperately needed in our all
too narrow and dully conforming society.

The methods are certainly consistent with the great demand
for flexibility in schools; a demand that has been partly achieved,
and where partly achieved successfully achieved, by use of many
of the means we are now advocating. The child is not a receptacle
for facts but an individual, especially one who can respond and
act. Children need to make, create and act, and they should
learn during the process of fulfilling these needs. One should
not so much be forcing the facts in as bringing out and encouraging each child's inherent ability. This view is consistent
with the use of programmed instruction, on the usual question-
and-answer basis. The basic syllabuses can be efficiently covered
for examination purposes, and more time is left as a result to
build up the individuality of the child, and to stimulate his
inherent curiosity and creativity. That syllabuses themselves need
to be continually overhauled we take for granted.

The use of the Dalton plan and programmed instruction, as
well as other audio-visual aids, also means that time is available
in which one can emphasize the interdependence of knowledge.
This is one feature which is missing from most school education
today. If education is really to have any success in the future
then this must be a new minimum requirement. The need is
more for understanding principles than for finding out facts.

The classroom, of course, for all its faults, possesses some
advantages. For example, class discussion and the sharing of ideas
are important. What will happen here is that what we might call
"flexible grouping" will be used for part of the time. This means
that classes can continually be formed and broken down into
ever-changing patterns designed to bring together, at the right
moment, those individuals who have reached the right stage and
have either the same or suitably contrasting interests. This is

perfectly consistent with the Dalton plan. It does, of course, though, make great demands on the organizational skill of the school. This again we should expect, and predict computer-controlled school administration, probably on an area basis.

It will be remembered that most school examinations are not very difficult, and full advantage will be taken of this to ensure, by the methods of tomorrow, that examinations will be easy hurdles to cross, until such time as they are wholly replaced by continuous assessment; these changes will occur long before the end of the century.

It is vital that the real education of the child, whether boy or girl, and the schools of tomorrow should all be co-educational, and should not be sacrificed to the mere passing of examinations. The passing of examinations has often been achieved at the expense of understanding and insight. Such unpleasant machine-like methods are precisely the opposite of what we are planning. But just as the rigid classroom system is doomed, so too is the examination system. We must act soon but with suitable circumspection.

It is not our wish to labour the ills of existing educational systems, but it is obvious that examinations have been passed in many cases by teaching the children merely how to manipulate symbols, and to write adequate answers to questions, *without* any real understanding of what it is they are doing. Our aim is not to produce students who are able to pass examinations two or three years earlier by better teaching methods, the aim is to ensure that the student passes the examinations, where examinations are still used, in plenty of time, with a greater understanding and insight which will stand him in good stead later in the educational system and life; what after all is education all about?

We should mention here the fact that where programmed instruction, or indeed any other individualized form of instruction, is introduced into a classroom, the effect is almost always to disrupt the class. Immediately the apparent "sameness" of the group is changed beyond all recognition, and the brightest of the students begin to get ahead of the rest. This causes great administrative difficulties if you try to make flexible individualized education fit into standardized classroom procedures.

Here we see a ray of hope. The effect of science and automation is generally to standardize and overcontrol; here we see in the vital field of education a chance for science and automation to breed individuality and amplify the differences between students.

The flexibility involved in the school of tomorrow will allow us to indulge a measure of encouragement for a child's achievement at each stage. We want to use the feedback of a "pat on the back" for a job well done. This is because schedules are set up at intervals of time which tell the student exactly what has to be achieved by the end of the specified time; if he achieves more than is necessary or achieves the scheduled limits before the end of the time, he is allowed to broaden and deepen his understanding by a certain amount of free, though guided, reading or other project. Where the child has achieved his scheduled standard in a certain subject, there are three possibilities open to him. He can go to another subject whose schedule is incomplete, and in which the child is getting behind, or he can go on in depth in that particular subject by carrying out a supervised project. The third possibility is that he can go on to some other activity altogether, with a non-curriculum subject, or an optional subject, or be allowed to work in the art-room or science workshop.

The responsibility for the decision as to which step should be taken will rest with the teacher, now turned tutor, in consultation with the child. Where the student *fails* to achieve the necessary schedule level, he is either subjected to greater constrained tuition, if this is made necessary by his lack of understanding, or he is automatically penalized and allowed less freedom by virtue of the fact that he has not been working sufficiently hard.

We must add a number of subjects, even though in very elementary form, to those normally provided by preparatory schools to help the above "carrots" to achieve their full rewarding effect. These subjects should at least include semantics (meanings), logic (ability to reason), philosophy (ability to speculate consistently) and sociology (ability to understand the patterns and relationships of people in society). They are not to be introduced explicitly as separate disciplines; rather they should be woven into the manner in which the English language and mathematics are taught. It is important, and obviously so, that an understanding of language, logic and the more abstract modes of thought should be acquired by boys and girls. It is as a result of this that deeper understanding of the ordinary routine subjects arises.

The aim throughout this plan is to develop the ability to show insight into problems, often of an abstract nature, before rather than after the actual manipulation of symbols occurs—whether mathematical symbols or languages. It is absolutely necessary in a successful educational system that the insight should go with the manipulation, where the manipulation is essential to achieve the necessary syllabus by a particular time; but at the same time intuition, insight and the development of the ability to discover facts for oneself must be developed over and above the requirements of the syllabus. And this will be achieved by motivating the child to do this for himself, and not by forcing him through the threat of punishment. The object will be to develop in the child a keen interest and sense of curiosity and discovery in the world in which he lives and a confidence in his own abilities. This is really only bringing out what is natural to him. Most schools today succeed only in stifling such a sense of curiosity and wonder.

We shall waste no time arguing about the extent to which existing schools perpetrate all the worst features that we have implied. All that matters is that we know now where we are going and where we must go in education, and we also know how to get there. There will, of course, be all sorts of variations on the basic pattern we have described. We cannot discuss these variations for different age groups and special schools for backward and handicapped children. This becomes too vast a subject. All must and will be catered for, and appropriate scientific methods will be developed for testing and selection so that a child starts with a far better chance of finding his right educational niche.

Our teacher of the future, we have said, will be a tutor. In fact, he will also need many of the skills of the psychiatrist. He will be responsible for the social life of the pupil and will try to provide a suitable environment. This takes us beyond the immediate problem of school in the narrow sense to school in the broadest possible sense. The emphasis in teaching is on an individual teaching himself and being supported by proper library facilities and a highly flexible organization.

But some schools will still have boarders and others have day boys and the social life of the school has still to be catered for. Here there is a need for grouping. For the purposes of sport and other social activities, boys and girls will organize themselves under the careful guidance of their teachers.

We would suggest that the next overall step needed in the development of the school is to split it up into five two-year groups, the sixth form school, or junior university, coming at the end, and being led up to by the introductory school, the junior school, the transition school, and the fifth form or senior school.

Children are growing up more quickly and require to be treated as adults earlier, and the methods of the better universities must be gradually brought into the schools and allowed to seep down from the seniors to the smallest juniors. This fits precisely with the Dalton type of scheme which allows different age groups to mingle in different schools according to their progress in the subject, while partly—although certainly not entirely—segregating them socially, and allowing primarily marginal overlaps of age groups.

Looking a bit further ahead, it is clear that in the likely event of the break-up of the family as a unit, the problem of providing a suitable social environment becomes even more acute.

The same problem applies to all aspects of life. The state, or some representative of the state, must decide on the extent to which interference or control of people is necessary. This is a familiar theme, and we must be careful here to ensure that representation of the children themselves is involved; state control could be the beginning of the totalitarian wedge we most fear. Should children, as boarders say, be completely controlled? For that matter, should employees in an industry have their employers cater wholly, or almost wholly, for their leisure? The difficulties and inherent dangers of such matters can hardly be overemphasized. It seems certain though that the children, students and employees of tomorrow are to be increasingly involved in systems of collective bargaining.

The old idea that an employer or even a schoolteacher is entitled to say exactly how an employee is to be treated or a child is taught is now becoming outmoded. Nothing would precipitate the most dangerous features of this situation more quickly than the decay of the family, even though that is precisely what is threatened. Even with the retention of the family unit, there will still be an inevitable increase in collective bargaining.

The most absurd omission from our educational system, which is only now being remedied, is sexual education. It seems strange that in life most skilled activities are known to need tuition. Yet sexual activity as practised by men and women is a considerable skill if performed properly. Surely then proper instruction is needed. We may also expect that education will be as much concerned with educating the emotions as with the intellect. Fuller artistic and musical appreciation is certain to be a feature for future development.

With the development of full sensory communication methods, such educational techniques will be taken for granted. Already we hear of teaching machines that work on touch, taste and smell, as well as by audio-visual means. Here it is the development of the needs which makes the need for the techniques obvious.

Education for leisure is one of the final steps towards total education, and this will provide education in the home for all.

We are entering the cybernetics age and our hopes are pinned to a great extent on education, and for all ages, and from birth to death.

The educational systems of tomorrow must allow permanent access to institutions of learning. We need education of the emotions, in sex, in social development, as well as in the basic subjects of human knowledge.

We especially need to teach an awareness of the world, its evolution and the tremendous problems that face us. Above all, we need to make that education as free as possible of brain-washing and the fear of totalitarian control, and this requires a permanent surveillance by independent adjudication on an international scale. It also means education must be primarily concerned with telling people how to find things out for themselves.

8 The Academic World

"He sups off silver dishes
And drinks in a golden horn.
But he will wake a wiser man
Upon the Judgment morn."

"I am a Gilly of Christ"
G. K. Chesterton

THIS CHAPTER is the second of two that attempt to tackle the problem of education and the emergence of new ideas in the background of our human evolution.

Almost everyone accepts the fact that education is vital to all human development, but most of us, some of whom have been closely associated with education, know the difficulties of actually putting education into evolution. It is not at all an easy task within the context of the present static social structure of the western world.

In a sense, in talking of the academic world, we are not talking primarily of education. We are talking rather of institutions which carry out research, influence the community with new ideas, while at the same time attempting to provide a continuity of teaching facilities, enabling others to join the ranks if they possess the necessary ability; the necessary ability, at least in theory, is to have new ideas and carry out original research, mostly within the ivory towers.

The background of universities is monastic. Oxford and Cambridge are direct offshoots of monasteries, and Yale and Harvard are offshoots of Oxford and Cambridge. Most of the earlier universities of the western world, though, also have monastic origins.

The university as an institution has been a most successful

feature of civilization. Without it, it is difficult to imagine the emergence of any civilization as we know it today. But since one of our basic tenets is that change is inevitable and adaptation to change is essential, we might ask whether universities have the necessary adaptability for the future, as change accelerates.

Universities are a social institution devoted to learning and discovery. They once catered for the wealthy and privileged alone, and gave a social stamp to a young man's education—women at this time hardly qualified for education at these dizzy heights—and also provided a secluded setting in which new ideas and abstract thoughts could be incubated.

A new type of modern university has recently emerged and is sometimes called a multiversity; to some, it is best illustrated by the University of California at Berkeley, and to some such a university more nearly resembles a factory, where the methods of mass production are far too much in evidence; whatever the truth, at least such changes show an attempt at realistic integration between universities and the communities they serve.

The idea that monks serve a community outside themselves or God may seem silly; the same therefore may be said of universities, if our analogy holds. The answer is that the analogy does not hold. Today universities are subsidized by the state.

We now come face to face with the fundamental question of what is the proper function of a university. It must be to serve the community, which itself is responsible for financing the university. This is not to say that it should concentrate wholly on short-term considerations, but it must commit itself to some extent to serve its community as well as further human knowledge and help, as all education should, to make human beings human. This is, of course, a sort of tightrope and naturally we might easily lose our balance and fall.

In America, a university education has for a very long time been much more universal than it is in Britain. The price of that universality has been an inevitable lowering of standards.

In Europe (until recently) too few people have attended university, and in Britain, as J. D. S. Bernal pointed out, fewer people proportionately speaking went to university in the 1930's than in most other European countries.

A report published in the summer of 1968 shows very clearly

the recent development of student members attending British universities. In the year 1965–66, according to the report, Britain had 170,000 full-time students attending universities. In 1953–54 it was 80,000, and back in 1938–39 it was 50,000.

During this period, particularly between the two most recent dates, the number of universities was greatly increased, especially by the upgrading of technical colleges and colleges of advanced technology. This, though, does not alter the basic fact that numbers have increased dramatically. This can be taken as symptomatic of the emergence of a new society and some awareness of the nature of that new society. It must also be regarded as grounds for encouragement.

Another set of figures which was published at the height of the student riots in Paris in the summer of 1968 was as follows. In the ten years from 1958 to 1968, the American university population went from 2,600,000 to seven million. In West Germany there were 110,000 students in 1950 and 250,000 by 1968. West Germany anticipates doubling this figure by 1980. In France there were 200,000 students in 1961 and by 1968 this number had risen to 515,000. Finally, in Britain, according to these figures, there were 216,000 in 1962 and by 1968 there were 418,000.

The apparent discrepancy in the above figures as far as Britain is concerned arises because the earlier figures are for universities alone and all the other figures are for all forms of higher education.

A university, by its teaching, gives continuity to what we believe necessary to pursue knowledge and help the search for truth, in every sense of these phrases. More important perhaps, and also more obviously a part of the current evolution of the university, it supplies a large number of technically qualified people to fill the increasing demand for posts in industry, commerce, government and indeed virtually all walks of life.

The evolution of the university system in Britain has brought it more into line with America. The same advantages and disadvantages are underlined. Here we have higher and even higher academic qualifications on paper, without comparably greater insight and ability in many of the more demanding applications.

The criticism here is that of an examination system and an

educational system that tend to be fact-filling rather than insight-building. The answer is, as we said in the last chapter, that we have not yet found a really satisfactory alternative to the examination system, which means that we await the results of present experimentation. We must, though, also hope for a change of heart among educationalists at all levels.

By the end of the century, our present experiments must have borne fruits. We shall judge people vocationally and select people by systematic and scientific means. This is an extremely complicated matter. It is also a matter which we must monitor closely since it is another possible example of an overcontrolled society. We do not want all our people to be like Pavlov's dogs.

At the moment there are vocational guidance services which tell you whether you are a *round* or *square* peg. They tell you a great deal more besides and with some measure of reliability. Psychological testing is much more sophisticated than it was thirty years ago, although there is obviously room for further improvement. In the future such tests will probably be carried out by the electroencephalogram (EEG), which records brain waves and will have far greater diagnostic power. That power must be used for ensuring the number of misfits is minimized, but not to actually condition people into being square or round pegs.

At the moment the holes in the community in which the pegs are to be stuck are advertised by journals, newspapers and the labour exchange amongst others, and represent a community in which the demand is greater than the supply. This will change with automation, cybernation and general scientific advance, and the time will come when the qualified will have to fight to obtain work, not because of the pay, which they will receive anyway, but for the privilege of working. The sort of fight entailed is like one frequently engaged in today to get a place in a first-class football team or theatrical group in Britain, or baseball team in the United States.

The falling off of work, in the sense we know it now, leaves our diagnostic methods to be used for other purposes such as deciding who is most deserving of the larger share of theatre tickets or cruises, and this we must stop at all costs.

Our ability to countercontrol in the manner of the current

trade unions will diminish as work diminishes, so one thing we must bend our efforts to is the need for "balancing movements" in the need for maintaining a "balance of power". Inefficiency has been our main hope so far and this is what is changing with the advance of science. Organized inefficiency may become one of science's major contributions to our future.

In the future, with the gathering information explosion comes also the documentation explosion. This documentation must be coded into large stores under computer control. It must exist on grounds of efficiency, since some measure of efficiency is vital, but must not stifle us with more paperwork for filing.

We see here quite clearly again the dangers of control—of downright totalitarian government springing from the ability to exercise complete control—though the fight between efficiency and injustice will continue. Students today as never before recognize the need to establish the voice of the rebel, largely to deter, or at least postpone, the autocratic voice of a fascist style of authority working in the name of efficiency, and often using with great effectiveness the very methods of science which have been so painstakingly developed with totally different applications in mind. But let us take a look at university life.

Universities today are usually divided into faculties or schools, which are themselves divided into departments. A science faculty may have departments of physics, chemistry, zoology, botany, psychology, physiology, etc. An arts faculty has English, French, history, geography and the like, where mathematics will often, like philosophy, appear in both arts and science, and the same is often true of economics and sociology; sociology, though, is more usually now to be found in the social science faculty with psychology, psychiatry and allied subjects. The classics still exist, sometimes in their own faculty, but sometimes under the banner of the arts faculty. We then also have the medical faculty, the legal faculty, the theological faculty and perhaps others besides.

Moving upwards from the faculties we find the various boards dealing with higher degrees, administration and representing the heads of departments. Also there is Senate which, with Council, forms the highest level of academic administration. Most of the people involved are amateur administrators, although some few, including the vice-chancellor himself, are full-time and to be regarded as professional. Also there are outside representatives, often from large local business organizations, who are strictly professional; these are usually members of Council, which is really the highest non-academic administrative body.

The chancellor of the university is usually something of a figurehead but may, if he is especially academically-minded, take an active interest in the university, and then at the other end of the hierarchy we find the departmental staffs, with some representation at the higher levels but whose main outlet is at departmental meetings. Below these come postgraduate students and the undergraduates themselves. The undergraduates are, supposedly, of course, the reason for the whole thing in the first place. In recent years, though, the emphasis has, at many universities, shifted more and more to research.

More often than not, the administration of universities is carried out by faculty boards, which were appropriate to smaller and more personal universities where the number of undergraduates and postgraduates together could still be counted in their hundreds. This same organization usually still operates today, where the same administrative methods are dealing with—or attempting to deal with—not hundreds but thousands of undergraduates and postgraduates; many universities have, as we have seen, increased in numbers by a factor of ten in the last thirty years. Coupled with so much amateur administration, the result is a good deal of wasted time without achieving the highest level of organizational efficiency.

American universities tend more often than not to have full-time deans, who are like many vice-chancellors in Britain. They are made deans for their supposed administrative skill rather than their academic standing. The effect is to provide slightly greater efficiency at the expense of slightly less departmental freedom. We are thoroughly aware of the dilemma implied; we may be more efficient, but sometimes it may be at the cost of freedom. While this is so, and hence our support for E.M. Forster's *Two Cheers for Democracy*, as well as frequent encouraging references to inefficiency, we must express the view that much more efficiency could still be achieved in university administration without paying any price in loss of freedom. Calculated freedom with minimum control and good selection is the necessary recipe.

The selection of university staff is carried out by an appointment committee. This committee does its best to fit the round peg to the round hole. It functions as efficiently as most selection systems, but the yardstick used is nearly always one of the standard or first degree obtained by the student and the candidate's research potential. In other words, the standard is almost wholly concerned with one's specialist subject. Not only does the problem of specialization rear its head here, but one is made acutely aware that absolutely no attention is paid to teaching skill.

The truth is that universities usually supply antiquated teaching standards. Even the introduction of a tutorial system on the lines of Oxford and Cambridge at provincial universities has not always helped. All too often, and this sometimes applies at Oxford and Cambridge, the tutorial becomes just another lecture.

The older universities have one great advantage. Partly because they are divided into colleges and partly because the tutorial method usually works better there—this is partly a matter of student–teacher ratio—the student is, at least usually, left to decide for himself what lectures he wishes to attend. Thus it is that the many dons who whisper and are, as a result and naturally enough, incapable of being heard, or are utterly unintelligible even when heard, or write everything at length even though in a manner which is utterly unreadable, or are just so unspeakably dull that they induce suicidal tendencies, all of them can be avoided. This freedom is not always available at other universities.

Lectures are really a thing of the past. Certainly lectures as staple diet are a thing of the past. Closed circuit television systems, films and programmed instruction are the most effective ways of transmitting basic and necessary facts. Furthermore, to be able to press a button and hear a lecture by someone who is both a good speaker and also internationally famous, and this combination sometimes occurs, is a matter that is now technically easy to arrange.

From all that has already been said, as well as from what was said in the last chapter, it will be seen that there is an urgent need to overhaul our university system. The effect of the vast increases in numbers is the prime cause of the need for revision. The increases have strained the existing methods to breaking point and destroyed the personal quality once enjoyed by the undergraduate.

Another aspect of this same question also finds our universities wanting; wanting on the score of social requirements. The bulk of university staff are lacking in worldliness. A university education is primarily intended to make people human. They are supposed by such means to express themselves to the full as human beings in a well-rounded way. They are also supposed to acquire vocational training; they are to become physicists, bacteriologists or classicists. The fact of specialization here stands in the way of the possibility of continuing with the old idea of a university. Knowledge was once a total thing that any person could, in principle, achieve. Certainly the combination of a broad vision coupled with some specialist knowledge was sufficient for most purposes until recently. But now none of this will do. You are expected to be a superspecialist and a worldly human being at the same time, and this is very nearly impossible.

Let us return now to take up the difficult question of selection in this vexed context of specialization. It starts at school. Schools are more typical reflections of the society they serve than are universities. This is not surprising since schools cater, and this was far more true in the recent past, for the vast bulk of the community and not just the select few. Schools, therefore, effectively hold the mirror up to society and provide what is thought to be needed. The result is that the superficial ends of most of western society become very obvious. The "successful" child has social success, and this is mirrored by sporting and athletic success on the one hand and sexual success on the other. The natural habitat for such success can be both metaphorically and literally the cocktail party.

The truth is that we in western society, which means especially Western Europe and North America, have, for altogether too long, held out the carrot of the cocktail party and all it implies as the totally appropriate and laudable goal and all that we should aim at. Even C. P. Snow's view that all the happy and serene men he had met had been sexually satisfied does not entail that we should accept sex via the success of sport and the cocktail party as an adequate and sufficient goal in and of itself; and here we are talking of the present day.

One particular effect that this western philosophy has had should not go unnoticed. At universities in both America and Europe, there are people who are extremely able at sport and have been thought to be stupid at work not because they were, in fact, stupid, but because success in one sphere made them less interested in success in another. Exactly the same thing happens at school. The majority of children are encouraged to be socially successful since this is believed, perhaps rightly, to be the appropriate copy of life. Success, especially social success, at school means success in life.

The boys who while at school find themselves unable to produce the necessary success in school's delicately balanced social and sexual life must find a substitute activity, which they do. They become the form's prizewinner and carry off the intellectual trophies which are regarded by the majority as being "second best". If you are successful at absolutely nothing then you are likely to become either a well-balanced person or a neurotic.

At university, the odds swing more in favour of the "second best", since by the very process of natural selection more of those that have these goals are present there. Even here sport is favoured and social success has clearly joined hands with sexual success. So the production of some of our finest brains is in the hands of people who are not well-rounded; they are not successful by the standards of the western world, and are, by definition, unworldly. It is these people who will inhabit the corridors of academic power for the next two generations, and understanding this there can be no need to complain of difficulty in understanding why universities have their problems; perhaps the most surprising thing is that their problems are not greater than they are.

We now trace our steps back again to the spectre of specialization. Most university staffs are dedicated to academic activities, and this primarily means research. They are well suited to a world which by the very nature of the information explosion ensures that more and more people must know more and more about less and less. This provides a genuine problem for a university. They are working with unpromising material in most unpromising circumstances.

By the end of the century, because of the further vast increase in knowledge, we shall have solved this problem by grading or streaming people according to their degree of specialization. There is a view sometimes voiced now which suggests we separate research from teaching, and this view will eventually carry the day. We shall not separate institutions according to whether they teach or do research, but we shall recognize that teachers and researchers can all too rarely be the same individuals.

A university department of the future will be answerable directly to the overall administration, cutting out the faculty or school stage which presently intervenes. The department will have representatives at different levels, some superspecialists, some specialists and some broad interpreters, whose skill lies mainly in linking the departmental research to other research activities in departments dealing with related subjects.

We have already sufficiently made the point that research is the yardstick by which university staff are currently selected and assessed. Teaching is an additional feature, but usually thought of as an irrelevancy, which sets the scene for the discontent which stems from a combination of administrative inefficiency and badly outdated methods of teaching, coupled with unworldly and unrealistic approaches to young people; this is the internal problem, and it is mixed up with the fear of too much control and the consequent loss of freedom.

The position is made much worse by the fact that more and more people are now attending university, and as a result the intake is no longer the unworldly few seeking a life substitute but the many, some of whom are concerned with the practical problems of changing the face of our society.

We can see easily that the sickness that is currently cast over western universities is bound to infect the schools, who are desperately trying to satisfy university entrance requirements. This attempt to satisfy university entrance requirements determines the manner in which schools are run and destroys what would otherwise be a sensible educational system. This is not quite true. The system would be a good deal better if it were not for universities, but one is forced to admit that it was anyway debased in some measure by "cocktail party" standards. But perhaps in the shadow of the fear of efficiency we should not make too much of this, even perhaps mildly applaud it.

The myth of education, especially of higher education, is much like the myth of running a successful business on a nine-to-five basis; it just does not work. We say one thing and do another. What we say is not very sensible but what we do is often absurd. Universities have become depersonalized and rigid in outlook and inefficient in practice. This is to put the matter in general terms, since many universities are, in fact, exciting, experimental and forward-looking; they, though, in 1970 are the exception rather than the rule.

In these internal circumstances alone there is enough material to provide some justification for the riots which in 1968 spread from California to Essex, through Europe by way of Paris, Prague, Madrid and Rome, and came to London in 1969. In fact such riots are not caused simply by internal university conditions. There are many other dissatisfied groups in society and the rioter in the university quickly becomes a leader of discontent for all people. It is natural that he should be the spearhead of a movement which carries with it thousands of malcontents and troublemakers, all helping to bring about a state of anarchy. These people could be regarded as the power that stops the encroachment of autocracy and dictatorship, so we shall have to ask ourselves whether we should not encourage, or at least not too actively discourage, such movements. We should perhaps rather try to channel their activities to more constructive ends, using more peaceful means, but even in this we are blunting one of the very spears that protect our freedom.

Apart from the wider implications of the university as a cradle for ideas—some people refer to them as a hotbed of discontent—there is the question of the actual production of academic ideas. Scientific discoveries which have emanated from universities have, more than any other single factor, changed the whole of civilized life. The splitting of the atom by Rutherford at Cambridge and the origination of cybernetics by Wiener at the Massachusetts Institute of Technology spring to mind immediately as examples.

More recently, we have seen the results of the scientific research work by Crick, Watson and Wilkins on the structure of the gene. This work, which has earned all three a Nobel prize, has given us the insight we need into the structure of life. This was a magnificent piece of scientific research and is one example of many where complicated apparatus was not extensively used. The imagination and abstract skill were used and it was the imaginative flair of the people involved which made their success possible.

It should be noticed in passing that Crick and Watson, like many other scientists, did not get on particularly well socially. It would be foolish not to readily appreciate that at universities as well as in most other social organizations where human beings work together they will quarrel and be jealous of each other. Some people are modest, but some are most immodest. Some people talk too much and some talk too little. It is all part of the human condition, and scientists are not better at mixing, nor nicer people to meet, than those to be found in any other social group; in fact they are often rather less so.

As to the subject matter of universities, this is rapidly undergoing a seachange. At the moment, though, we are plagued by a number of chunks of knowledge or myths which do not fit comfortably into our accepted categories. We must then simply change our categories. The whole burden of our discussion of change, adaptability and flexibility has been to make clear that all plans, all systems and all organizations must either adapt to change or banish. If they do not as institutions vanish, then society itself does.

At the moment we are bothered by all sorts of ill-assorted interests such as extrasensory perception, water-divining, hypnosis, psychedelics, and a whole host of other things for which a home is not readily available. Research workers cannot ignore such matters merely on the grounds that they do not happen to fit in with their theories. The problem is how best to maintain suspended judgment in certain cases, reject others and accept yet others.

The academic world lives like a bridge between the child and life, and leaves, at least in Britain, a gulf between itself and the world of business. It is this business world which is the subject of our next chapter.

9 The Business World

"The disparity between the rich and the poor has been noticed.
It has been noticed, most acutely and not unnaturally, by the poor.
Just because they have noticed it, it won't last for long, Whatever
else in the world we know survives to the year 2,000, that won't."
                                "*The Two Cultures: and a Second Look*"
                                                        C. P. Snow

WE ARE TEMPTED to call this chapter "The Myth of Big Business",
where the myth lies mainly in the idea of its superefficiency.
No one questions the existence of—or the need for—the
business world, but one may question its efficiency, and the
answer, we have already suggested, may lie in a sense of relief at
its inefficiency.

Just as schools and universities are typical human social
institutions, so is the business house, be it small—even a single
shop—or a large chain of stores, something of the size of
General Motors, I.B.M. or, as some cynic has said, the Roman
Catholic Church.

The comment on the Church is a comment on the fact that
power often resides in any large organization, purely on account
of its size. Just as wealth lies in the United States of America
partly on account of its size and partly as a result of its enormous
natural resources, so power is usually vested in the possession
of enough, or more than enough, of what is needed in the
marketplace. Such natural resources would not, though, be a
source of wealth to America had it not arrived at the stage
where it could develop and utilize that wealth effectively. It is
rather like harnessing the potential power of a large waterfall.
You have to be able to build the dam to utilize effectively the
power. Such a state of affairs presupposes a society which is

already technologically advanced and must depend on the educational and other facilities available in the community. Awareness of this fact of life has steadily increased, and is reflected in the situation where many large firms now regularly endow university professorships and give money to education, as well as build their own training and educational colleges. It has taken a long time to achieve this state of affairs and even now many firms pay no more than lip service to education.

There are many reasons which are deep-rooted in British society which explain the reluctance on the part of business people to accept the need for much formal education. In the first place, many of our most successful businessmen and industrialists have come up "the hard way" via the factory floor, and are justly proud of their success. This success is particular to the business and may often later be found to be a disadvantage in the broader horizons encountered as a director of many different firms. The really great men of business will be successful in any event, just as the brilliant scholar will thrive irrespective of the school he is sent to or the university he attends. The successful businessman who received his training within an industry and with little formal education will tend to feel disparaging about the need for schools and universities. This feeling will receive a great deal of encouragement from his experience, particularly of university graduates, who all too often will not be successful in business. Worse still in the eyes of the successful and dedicated businessman, they will often appear to be wholly disinterested in the profit-making success of either the business as a whole or any particular part of it.

The trouble is that our educational system has only recently made mild noises of acceptance in the direction of the business world. Until relatively recently business was thought unclean and profit-making as a goal faintly disgusting.

In much the same way science and engineering were, and in some ways still are, thought to be ugly; the idea of oily fingers is not an acceptable accompaniment to the finger bowl. But this uncomfortable relationship of education to business certainly does not apply in anything like the same way in America. There they have much more practically geared their educational system to the real needs of the community. We must, after all, accept the fact that some people have to work at dirty and boring jobs if we are to survive in the present competitive economic world, at least until automation itself performs the tasks for them. The world we shall now take a brief look at is the so-called "professional business" world.

Broadly speaking, people who do not go into professions go into business. It is not that all business people are without professional qualifications, nor are we suggesting a clearcut distinction between professional and business people. There is indeed a whole group of people who go into the civil service or the armed services, or become policemen and firemen, and perform other roles in what is sometimes called the "public sector"; they do not fit easily into our broad classification, but are something of a compromise between the two.

We are concerned with business, as we have said, all the way from the small privately owned shop to the huge publicly owned business and the nationalized corporation. We are concerned with businesses that sell both at the retail level and at the wholesale level; we are concerned with businesses that sell as manufacturers and also those that sell a service.

We live in a community, and this applies in much the same way to the whole of the western world, which buys and sells and works for a living in the marketplace.

Buying and selling can vary from the farmer supplying his goods in the market to the retailer buying the goods; a reasonable and fair relationship may exist throughout. Some "sharp practice" exists at all levels and among all types of people, but by and large with personal contact and with a situation of mutual advantage to both parties trading can be, and usually is, fair. Difficulties arise in business for various reasons. In the first place, the occurrence of ignorance and naivety encourages one side to take advantage of the other. In the second place, the business may become depersonalized in the same way as schools and universities.

The trend towards depersonalization is everywhere apparent in our lives today and this trend will continue, but as it does, we must remodel the organization of our society to make up where possible for the damage that is done.

Let us now have a closer look at the problem of depersonalization as we find it in business—nearly always big business. In a large organization you may find yourself employed by a firm that does not appreciate the importance of personal relationships or cannot provide the necessary organization to achieve good personal relationships.

There are many examples of some of the biggest firms both in Britain and America that circulate messages to their staff reassuring them that "they are not mere cogs in a massive impersonal machine", when all the time they (the cogs) are completely aware that they are just that. From where they sit they can see a hundred or more other cogs in the same depersonalized system, which is in any case structured so inefficiently that no one is in proper personal contact with others either above or below him in the hierarchy. Needless to say, this is the wrong sort of inefficiency.

Everyone knows of firms, large and profitable, who treat the bulk of their employees as an army of privates and NCO's, with a clearcut social ramification which allows eating only in the correct dining-room or mess; the dining-room must be the one for your particular rank. This in itself is not necessarily such a bad thing if it were an isolated matter. Unfortunately, more often than not it is symptomatic of a rigidly stratified system where the attitude at best tends to be benevolently dictatorial and at worst can be unbearably autocratic.

There are many old jokes about military service life which can be applied to present commercial practice. "You are not paid to think but just to do what you are told." Unfortunately, when the firm implicitly follows such a line of thought, and especially where the salary scales are high and the company privileges extensive—free food and other merchandise—the result is to produce a group of people who lack all initiative; they become cowed and lacking in drive. In fact, they behave as if they were brainwashed.

This sort of deadening effect is obviously multiplied manyfold if the work to be done is intrinsically dull, as it often is if mechanical production processes are involved. There is of course here a considerable saving grace in that such mechanical activities are most easily capable of being automated. So the human production lines of today beome the automated production lines of tomorrow.

Some of the Charlie Chaplin humour of *Modern Times* has passed into history. Automated production will change the nature of the whole production company of tomorrow. It will throw up its own psychological problems of loneliness and isolation which will not be to everyone's liking. Women, for example, are often content to form a human production line in simple activities such as putting stoppers on bottles, packing cigarettes and similar menial tasks. They thus permit themselves to be herded together so that they can talk and enjoy social contact and earn money in the pursuit of a job which requires no thought.

There is, of course, in 1970 a great deal of difference between the attitude of the woman and the man to work. A woman is employed, most generally, on a purely temporary basis waiting on marriage or some release from what is not as boring as it might be because of the social consolations and also because the bulk of such women are not highly educated. The fact that very few, if any, such jobs will be available by the turn of the century is amply compensated for by the fact that there will be only a few women whose education will have been so neglected.

A man, more because he is likely to be saddled with his job for a complete lifetime, is keen to find a job with good opportunities and one which is not intrinsically dull. Big business pays lip service to this ideal and achieves some limited success. The employer cannot be sure that only round pegs go into round holes, and this is especially true at a time of full employment, where you have often as an employer to offer a job to a person who is really quite unsuited to it. In the future, with absolutely minimal employment in the sense that we know it today, coupled with more sophisticated selection methods, the number of misfits must diminish almost to zero. Before rejoicing too quickly at this prospective advance, let us remind ourselves that the stripping of one layer off the surface of an onion leaves other layers; new discontents and problems are always bound to occur and are a part of what gives human beings drives and purposes without which they could not survive; it also reflects their adaptive capacities.

The biggest troublemakers in a community are those that are too able and too clever for the job they are asked to do and for the responsibility they are asked to take on; much less trouble comes from the person who lacks the necessary skill. A problem for tomorrow is that there will be a far greater tendency towards the first type of misfit rather than the second.

Any organization that has hopes of succeeding while still employing people will need to learn the basic principle that to employ people implies the need to provide personal contact. How is this to be done? A business gets bigger and bigger and inevitably more impersonal. We can break factories down into smaller factories but we still need to provide personal contact. Each member of the company must be answerable to someone who knows and understands him.

In whatever manner such a flexible chain of personal relationships is achieved, it certainly must be achieved. Furthermore, it must be based on small integrated groups. There are many recipes that have been suggested and some have from time to time been tried.

Perhaps it is unnecessary to say that knowing and understanding a person is a very demanding business and one that it is very difficult for a manager to achieve. Often we hardly understand our own motives and behaviour so we should expect to make mistakes in understanding those of other people. The manager indeed needs, like the schoolmaster and the university teacher, some of the qualities of the psychiatrist. These, of course, he will have within the next thirty years, since of all sciences psychiatry is one that must advance most of all. This is another aspect of control and communication.

Our subject of communication and control rears its head at every corner of our investigation. It is not coincidence that cybernetics has made such extensive progress in business. A business is like an organism that consumes its raw materials and produces goods or services and has to dispose of its waste products. This last point raises such major considerations as pollution; but we shall not discuss that here. A business must be flexible, dynamic and able to grow and learn in order to survive. If it does not have the characteristics which allow it to survive, and these must include adaptability to changing circumstances, then its destruction is assured.

Communication even in its simplest forms can be extremely bad in many large systems. Analyses have been carried out in various organizations such as the U.S. Army and several large corporations showing that information seldom flows easily down through a hierarchical structure and often never flows back up the hierarchy at all. Statements on notice-boards are not read, and are often in any case couched in terms which are either ambiguous or unintelligible. Viewed as an organism such a failure to communicate successfully among the internal organs of the system augurs badly for the survival of the whole body. The tradition of anti-intellectuality which is so common on the higher levels of big business is also no help. To shudder and make the usual facial gestures of incredulity at the use of words with more than two syllables fails the least exacting criteria of wit.

Witlessness in one thing often, though not always, implies witlessness in others. There is certainly a high correlation between the two. Here we must turn our thoughts back to science, logic and language. It is not only that we need scientific experts in universities, even more do we need them in industry; and indeed in politics and all walks of life the well-rounded person who understands science and scientific method. We need people who realize that science is refined commonsense and know that it is the application of such commonsense that makes any system efficient. If the arts and religion make it humane, then an intellectual tradition should be the very one to foster in the world of business. At the moment such an end seems remote, but by 2000 the relatively few beings employed in industry will be of the highest calibre. Work will be by the very nature of things more attractive by virtue of its scarcity and non-commitment.

We must not create the impression that business, especially big business, where the difficulties are greatest, provides problems which are in some way inferior to or easier than those encountered in research—scientific or otherwise—and in teaching people. Some of the most difficult scientific problems, to say nothing of psychological and sociological problems, are to be found in industrial settings. Furthermore, industry has many brilliant people who are able to solve such problems; we are, though, underlining the fact that too often it does not have the people with the necessary skill and, worse, the need for them is not even understood.

In the meantime, ignorance of simple logic and ineptitude over language, while comic at times, should not be tolerated. Too often in the narrow discipline of a business, especially the more impersonal larger business, we hear questions put with a "Yes" or "No" answer expected, even though it cannot logically be given. But then, of course, you are paid just to do what you are told and not to think.

The other absurdity so often perpetrated by men who are directors of large companies is to assert that some word that has become the bone of contention of the moment is clearly to have only one meaning. " 'Presently' means just what it says, it means presently." That in this case it happens to mean 'immediately' and in that it happens to mean 'in a few moments' is unknown to the asserter of the statement. Or worse, it is known but it happens to be convenient to suppress such knowledge.

Language comes up in our story again and again, and we have to let it do so implicitly with a series of reminders of its vital role in each and every context.

Language is used, by poets and writers, often like paint is metaphorically daubed on to canvas. Words, are, perhaps as a result, often referred to as mysterious. Certainly their evocations can be magical.

"Sweet to ride forth at evening from the wells,
Where shadows pass gigantic on the sand,
And softly through the silence beats the bells
Along the golden road to Samarkand."

But in business, words cannot in general be used in this poetic way to convey information. The trouble is that words can as easily be used to obscure issues as to clarify them, a fact well understood by many people, perhaps especially by advertising men, lawyers and politicians.

A word is a label which has what meaning we invest it with. We might, like Alice in Wonderland, pay our words more to do more. But they are still labels. The word 'pencil'—the word is in single quotation marks—is not the same as a pencil, which is made of wood, lead, etc. We use no single quotation marks for the thing as opposed to the word. A 'pencil' has six letters and a pencil can be used to write with. Words are ambiguous when used out of context and may anyway mean more than one thing. They are vague and subject to change of fashion and a thousand other vicissitudes that communication is heir to. This, you will remember, is precisely one of the things we wanted our educational system to cater for. We want the well-educated and well-rounded men running big business, not the proudly ignorant and congenitally unintelligent.

It may be timely to remind the reader who knows businessmen and businesses which are quite different from those hinted at that we are intentionally, as with education, dwelling on the worst in order to highlight the best. We shall blandly assert that more of the worst is available because of the lack of ability to change with the times. Success breeds rigidity and refusal to change, and it is the most successful companies that tend to survive and get bigger and bigger. Here if anywhere we must have a certain efficiency, since business is the lifeline of our capitalist economy. We must save our inefficiency—even plan it—for other aspects of our life.

The problem of science is much like that of language and logic. Awareness of the impact of science is gathering momentum. Many famous experiments have been carried out showing that personal interest in the work of the employee—easy in a small firm and especially when one is self-employed—is more vital than the physical conditions under which people work. You can improve or impair the environment, but as long as it is done pleasantly with at least the apparent desire to please, the output and standards of the employee improve.

Similarly, many experiments have been done showing that more work can be done in shorter periods of time than in longer periods. People get bored and cannot give their best all the time. This presents a genuine problem because it is not always easy to stimulate in the factory some motivation as in an Everest climber or a football player. You need, though, something like that degree of determination and something like that sort of teamwork. Although it is not possible in every type of business, one step that could sometimes be taken is to free the employee from the nine-to-five routine. At universities it is understood that people cannot have ideas to order. It is realized that they are sufficiently keen to work at their own best time. Much of business could and indeed will, in time, be done in the same way. Careful selection and increased motivation in the coming age of leisure will make it possible to have many people work in their own time. To reject such an idea out of hand would be crass, and reflect a fatal lack of understanding of human psychology. Such a change will be made all the more possible by the elimination of dull routine jobs and higher standards of education at all levels. The main difficulty at the moment is the relative lack of interest intrinsic to the job. This is where the university man or professional scores because he is essentially subject-orientated and not job-orientated.

The level of discipline in a business surrounds time-keeping and assessment of work. In the future it will be entirely on assessment. This means the need for the development of clearcut and clearly communicated job objectives and clearcut criteria of success and failure. This must be done and will be done and at the same time we shall hope, by virtue of education, to eliminate the petty tyrant from the business scene.

In addition to all that we have said, it should be pointed out that one way of improving motivation on the part of the *employee* is to give him a stake in the business. He then has some of the satisfaction gained by working for himself. It is very surprising that such a simple method of increasing motivation has not been used more often.

The role of decision-taking at all levels is greatly simplified when criteria are clearcut. At the moment decisions are often taken in an ignorantly autocratic environment. Decisions are often taken in isolation by chairmen. These decisions are often ludicrously wrong because the chairman does not know the relevant facts. Many autocratically run companies have boards whose main purpose becomes that of concealing as many facts as possible. This is especially simple if the company has an easy profitable bread-and-butter line. The result is gross inefficiency, shown up clearly in such conditions as when they attempt take-overs and mergers.

One of the ways in which a business increases its size is by swallowing other businesses, and up to a point this is rather like a human being eating food and getting fatter and fatter. But the food must fall within a certain range; calories make for fatness, and if your aim is to increase weight then the foods with most calories are most needed. There is a parallel in "takeovers". In general terms, a takeover will not prove successful unless the firm carrying it through is especially equipped to take over a particular firm. It must have expert knowledge of the business and understand the ends and the means of the business to be taken over.

The counterargument usually made to the above is to say that business and management can be brought together. This is a fallacy in most circumstances, because although it may be desirable to buy management with the business, unless there is the necessary expert knowledge and sympathetic appreciation in the parent firm, the whole operation must fail. Here, as within business, the psychological factors are essential. You are taking over a business and you need to provide some continuity of management, even though you may take the opportunity to get rid of some of the least valuable or elderly directors on the old board. You are trying to get the best of both worlds; you are trying to provide a new image for the business and you are trying to provide continuity of management. You have to engage the loyalty of the new employees and you must, as a result, tread with extreme care. If the image of the acquired company is quite different from the parent, then you automatically encounter antagonisms. It is the same in personal relationships. You are inclined to say to your latest secretary or cook, "Sheila never did it that way", and such comments are nearly always harmful.

If you as a football team took over another football team, only a lunatic would expect it to immediately acquire the same colours, the same tactics and behave as if it had not a past of its own.

It is extremely difficult to take over another system successfully and almost as difficult to perform a satisfactory merger. All these things, though, have at times been done. The recipes for success are compatibility, flexibility and understanding.

Nationalization is, of course, one further step towards the construction of the primitive monster which cannot survive. The trouble is that nationalized industries must exist, since no

E

country can morally allow certain industries to be privately owned. Furthermore, if morality does not appeal as a reason, we can say no country can, for practical reasons, allow certain industries—particularly communication industries—to be run privately.

There is one consideration which we should mention and that is how business could cater for the coming evolution—in this case it may even be revolution. The point is that one may recommend new desirable states for a system, but unless you can also supply the methods for their achievement the recommendations may not be of much use.

The problem is how to cater for cutting down in people, especially the less qualified and higher paid. Already in 1970 we see the higher paid over-fifties being pushed into premature retirement and replaced by a less expensive younger man. This is bound to happen and we should copy the pattern of the armed forces and have people graded so that they can retire or be asked to retire at a series of points, say, at the age of 45, 50, 55, 60 or 65.

Appropriate pension schemes must be obligatory and the size of pension must relate to the age of retirement. We need only to extrapolate from these simple beginnings to have a graded scheme of payments for all people regardless of whether they have a job or not. This also paves the way for the future world where you will be paid for existing irrespective of whether you work or not.

Such a programme applies as much to nationalized industries as to private ones, and it is the former who are tending to take the lead.

The nationalized industry is often bad if it is a monopoly, just as monopolies are usually bad. But we are at the moment playing the international capitalist game, and have somehow to play it effectively if we are to survive; although we may have a version of internationalism by 2000. Such a "one world" will still be geared to state-controlled capitalism in the main. The lack of incentives in an international communist system as judged by what we have seen so far makes it unlikely to hold sway.

Our biggest danger in the immediate future remains in the direction of totalitarianism and autocratic control. An influential army officer class can be persuaded to autocracy when faced with extinction. In some ways industry is similarly placed. If faced with extinction by nationalism, which is the path the present pattern of bigger and bigger and fewer and fewer firms suggests, the reaction may be to fight. Just as the student world is in a fervour of unrest, so we may expect the same more positive unrest from industry. One hopes that it will not lead to fighting in the streets of all countries in the world, but it certainly could.

10 The Political World

"This is . . . a book of good faith. All the good faith and the goodwill of the world will be necessary in the next few years to save mankind from her worse self."

"Victors Beware"
Salvador de Madariaga

HOW WILL our new world of the immediate future, with automated education, greatly increased leisure and a new class structure, deal with the political matters, and what political matters will it deal with? We should have in mind the facts of the past and the present on one hand, and the methods of cybernetics on the other. We can clearly marry up these two aspects of our problem and produce both a short-term and a long-term recipe.

At the present time, the background of the Houses of Parliament is the university debating society. In much the same way the American Senate and House of Representatives is based on their own debating traditions of the past. We should perhaps be clear that no one is complaining of this tradition; in spite of a slight doubt that may linger the emotions play too large and logic too small a part, but even this doubt is countered by our desire for humanity and the preservation of a measure of inefficiency.

The plain fact is though that if, as we have claimed, all systems are in evolution, then political systems—perhaps especially political systems—can be no exception. The questions that arise are therefore those of goals, those of constraints imposed by other circumstances also in evolution, and the development and application of new methods.

The immediate goals must remain the same. These are to

provide an efficient organization to control and communicate with the community being served, and to do this efficiently.

The constraints, which imply change, lie largely in the vast development in communication and control methods. Let us consider the problem of communication first. This is obviously very much in flux. Today even at the level of the everyday citizen we have television, including satellite television, radio, newspapers and other more limited forms of quick communication. This necessarily suggests that in the future there will be no need for all members of either the House of Lords or House of Commons to be present during the full debating agenda, which is at present, at least in theory, demanded of them. This, of course, will apply to any job, any that is of the few "jobs" left to be done by human beings.

A number of different forces are working here and working in somewhat different directions. In the short term, the advantages of highspeed communication, which threatens to diminish the need for physical travel, also suggest that MPs, for example, can listen to debates while at other places—perhaps even on other planets—and even vote from a distance. On the other hand, the great increase in leisure activity which is also clearly coming suggests that a parliamentarian's role could be played far more completely than at the present. Parliamentarians would not, under these new circumstances of increased leisure, be pressed quite so hard as they are at the moment, by trying to work a system really designed for the nineteenth century: a century of leisure and debate. This is a similar point to the one made about universities. This suggests that politicians will become more professional, which is highly desirable; they could be the interpreters of scientific research, and will themselves have training in science and philosophy as well as economics and politics. This will enable them in turn to use scientific methods in their decision-taking.

The methods of election may well be changed. Proportional representation has enough to recommend it to be seriously considered. But whatever the outcome here, the need to have both local and national representation is obvious. The new computerized social system will surely call for a type of specialized and graded "Ombudsman" type of system that is likely to receive widespread approval as being a counterweight to the threat of depersonalized and centralized control. If we consider the question of communication again, we are reminded that it certainly could permit of the Member of Parliament spending more time in the area he represents.

Politics at the moment is, as we have agreed, geared to the debating society approach, where it is not so much the facts, or the logic about the facts, but the emotional appeal which is paramount; is this likely to change? And do we want it to? The answer hinges in part on the extent to which we can develop our political decision-taking procedures, but it seems clear that however far the man–machine phase of decision-taking goes towards the "machine only" phase, the human must fight to keep ultimate control, since also he is representing the human race, who must always retain human emotions; we must always retain some element of an emotional appeal. There is the fight to retain the family unit—since fight there should be—and this is a typical part of the fight against the complete control of reason without emotion.

It is often argued that there are fundamental differences between scientific, artistic, everyday and political decisions. An economist may recommend a certain step based on good economic evidence, but that step needs to be placed in a political context for us to make a final decision. Are these differences real or imaginary; if they exist, to what extent are they different from each other?

The answer cybernetics and science has is simple. Different decisions, and different data over which the decisions are made, can indeed occur at various levels of complexity, with various degrees of hunch involved, but above all they occur in different contexts.

The acceptance of different levels does *not*, however, mean that the total process of decision-taking cannot be taken into the computer context. The difficulty is that the vested interest of those currently making decisions is necessarily opposed to the idea of handing the work over to machines. Fortunately, there is no immediate danger of this happening because we are currently in the machine–man interaction phase of development, and this will continue for the better part of the decade, before the autonomous decision-taking machines and programs take over.

The day will certainly come when machines will take independent decisions, and perhaps we should now consider some of what this entails.

In the first instance, we should make clear that the evolution of man–machine to pure machine decisions comes about simply because the evolution of machine systems is so much faster than that of man systems; this is ironically due to the ingenuity of man.

Consider the dilemma of the human beings who are running the decision-making computer. What reason will they have for denying the validity of the machine decision? In the early days a very dedicated human being may give voice to doubts, but as the machine becomes more and more efficient, so inevitably the human being is bound to use the policy of "I stand to lose a lot if I challenge the machine decision and it is right (or at least I am wrong), and if I let the machine go ahead and it is wrong I cannot be blamed". Inevitably, machine decision-taking must come.

The conditions for satisfactory machine decision-taking include, among other things, the presence of a model of each source of information in the environment, indeed of the whole of the environment. It goes without saying that the model will appear in highly abstracted form such as language, logic, mathematics or diagrams. The test is, of course, whether the detail so retained in the computer is enough to make for sufficiently accurate decision-taking. More important by far, however, is the need to provide for the human beings against the possible totalitarian rationality of the machine. We must therefore prepare a ground for retreat in the form of whatever safeguards we can manage; this may mean the programming of humanlike emotions into the machine.

But as far as the rational model is concerned, a radar source of information or a human being could be earmarked by a simple number, the number being an index of the reliability of that source. The actual weighting of the reliability number could vary from some complex weighting to a simple count of how many times information given out by the source has been right and how many times wrong.

Whatever the complexities in the assessing of evidence and the degree of confirmation of a theory, some such procedure must be built into the machine and must itself be revised or otherwise in the light of some principle of confirmation.

Note next a special problem: inanimate sources of information are merely reliable or not according to their behaviour. This same argument does not apply to animate sources of information. Animate sources are capable of deception, they are capable of intentionally deceiving other people, or receivers of their information. Thus it is that our autonomous decision-taking computer could be "bluffed" unless it took steps to guard against it. The presence of an emotional system may here be extremely valuable in its contribution to rationality.

To explain briefly the position on bluffing, we have to remember that an "intelligent" computer, just like an intelligent person, must keep data about things and people in its environment. We sometimes say that it keeps *models* of the environment, and the models must also include one of itself. This is the dawn of consciousness or self-awareness.

In the internal models kept of inanimate things such as radar screens, we have an assessment of their efficiency in terms of, say, their previous record. In terms of human beings, we must also have a record of their efficiency on past occasions, but we must also have an estimate of their motive in saying or doing whatever they say or do at any particular time.

It is not easy to estimate when someone is trying to bluff you, but at least there are certain almost standard circumstances where the motive to bluff is obvious. "If I am trying to sell you something", "If I am trying to win your support in some campaign". The sort of circumstances are, on the whole, well known. All we can hope to do is to document such circumstances and weight the probabilities associated with belief in the relevant people accordingly.

Once again the complexities of human relationship are too great for us to make quickly explicit all the features of probability weightings (most human beings call such things "hunch" and "insight") which are needed to deal with this sort of circumstance. What we can say is that people are often the victims of confidence tricks, and therefore they themselves cannot have worked out "bluff-proof" formulae. This is obviously the case since the very fact of dealing with complicated probability weightings is an assurance of no certainty, and therefore of possible error.

The method adopted so far in dealing with bluffing at the computer level is, as we have said, to list all the circumstances where the motive to deceive may occur. Furthermore, as in the case of 2-person, 3-person and n-person games, so we find here the inevitable pressure of double-, triple- and n-tiple bluffs; once more the hierarchical structure of models of human intelligence is clearly shown.

Let us now return to the problems confronting the western world in the light of these decision-making developments. In the first place, it is clear that the larger the decision-making unit the better, since an integrated community must do better than an amalgam of competitors who are not working in the interests of the community as a whole.

This means that in Britain the next goal should be the setting up of a United States of Europe (USE). The Common Market negotiations are clearly a step towards this end, an end which is generally recognized to be in Britain's best ultimate interest.

America's interest must be the same as Britain's interest, and therefore must foster the idea of USE and also ensure the closest co-operation between the USA and USE.

As time goes by, it becomes increasingly clear that such a co-operative arrangement is also in the best interests of more remote countries such as Australia and India, who may wish to be associated with the western alliance. However, whether they do so, or see their future in alliance with another bloc such as Africa, the Soviet Union or China, is one of many questions we shall not attempt to answer. What we shall say, however, is that these steps—however taken—are all steps to "one world" and this still leaves open the future relations between that one world and other worlds; this is part of our colonization of space.

Politically, the bunker on each fairway is totalitarianism. Totalitarianism is the easy alternative that occurs when things are difficult to deal with or go wrong. The increased control that we shall be able to exercise on individuals and other individual and group opinion makes the danger of fascism greater than ever before. These dangers are, of course, precisely what Aldous Huxley, George Orwell, Samuel Butler and Sir Thomas More have warned us about. The development of science and cybernetics unfortunately increases the threat by providing more and more efficient methods of control by machine.

Fascism can come about as soon as one of two (or both) conditions is met. The first is that you know what is best for the community and the second is that you know how to impose that which is "best" on the community.

The problems of society are manifold and so complex that it would be idle, even absurd, to pretend that they can be easily clarified. We shall, however, look at two particular features which have at least an air of being reasonably clearcut.

The first feature is that of "unconscious causality". We do not easily accept the fact that what we do is contributory to a state of affairs that we may greatly regret. Rex Warner, in his novel *Why Was I Killed?*, makes the point that you may pursue apparently harmless ends and yet provide a situation as a result which is both harmful and precisely the opposite from the one you intended. This difficulty may arise for various reasons, and one reason only—this is what Rex Warner was concerned with—is that there is no connection recognized between what one does and what occurs as a result.

It is extremely difficult to foresee the exact results of one's actions, so that to sometimes bring about—or help to bring about—a situation which is the precise opposite of the one intended is not at all surprising.

We should remind ourselves yet again at this point of the fact that all learning and all intelligent activity is a direct function of what goals and subgoals are provided. These goals and subgoals may be changed, but while they exist they must be decisive in fashioning our behaviour. To this extent at least life, and this applies rather especially to political life, should be a search for goals and subgoals and an exploration of the best methods to achieve those goals. At the same time, we have to admit that ends and means cannot be wholly separated, so that what scientists, among others, develop by way of means determines in great measure the ends for which the means will be used.

There are branches of modern cybernetics that are particularly well equipped to help in analysing the relationship between the "best" goals and the "best" means of achieving them, and this carried out within the context of human needs and human emotions is precisely what we should encourage; we shall continue unavoidably to walk a tightrope in the development of science.

A second principle—one we have mentioned before—is that of "two cheers for democracy". The burden of the message is simple enough. You cannot have, while humans are human, a political system that is both wholly sympathetic to the individual and wholly efficient. The answer to this must lie in compromise, and it is democracy, among other things, that ensures that such a compromise is carried through.

The processes of politics must increasingly be made explicit by scientific means and humanized for human ends. We need to continue to try as hard as possible to separate ends and means, even if in the end the best we can hope for is a compromise. The rule by human beings in the future must be via the computer and not in spite of it. We shall have periods of machine–man interaction and periods where machines begin to dominate man, but whatever the route we shall at some time be brought to the point where we have to face squarely the fact that we as human beings are no longer dominant in the community; we have bred a superspecies. It must be a sympathetic and sophisticated superspecies; we must, as its forebears, ensure this.

The vested personal interest in political matters, as against a backcloth of large-scale international evolution, is such that we must expect radical changes.

Political people in the future may be the same as big businessmen, the same as academics, or better, some compromise between the two. But whichever way the evolution occurs the fact remains that the human beings involved are to be increasingly subjected to the pressures of a cybernetic age. Everything must be done scientifically; everything must be done by computer, or by machine and model, of a cybernetic kind.

The political system is one of the last to be attacked by our machine age, but attacked it will be and in the end may well fall. The result will be to place our future in the hands of science, and the sinister thing is that there appears to be no choice.

The short-term trap lies, and we must say it yet again, in totalitarianism, and this is the equivalent of unintelligent as opposed to intelligent science. It is narrow and parochial as opposed to broad and total in outlook. But it is also the result of the tremendous competitive pressures of human selfishness. We need, in other words, to have "eyes in the back of our head" if we are to survive the threat; and ironically science can supply those eyes. Science is both an angel in disguise and the nigger in the woodpile at the same time. Our problem is not what will happen but how, and how we can control the way it is brought about.

We have now to sound a further note of warning. So far we have hinted that educationalists, businessmen and politicians among other people are unscientific and rigid in attitude, and that they represent institutions which are rigidly traditional and incapable, or almost incapable, of evolving. All of this is in some measure true, but it also applies to the scientist himself, perhaps especially to the scientist.

We saw this danger in talking of research scientists in universities. They are often narrow and parochial in their attitudes. In fact there are many companies in which the operational research men or the computer men are among the most rigid-minded of all. After all, one can be rigid in many different ways. The author himself well remembers arguing on a television programme that any crime was forgivable—absolutely any crime! Then adding that one of the things I can *never* accept (forgive) are those people who are always apparently keen to condemn others. One other person in the programme kindly pointed out that perhaps understanding should be available to those who cannot forgive as well as those that do other unfortunate things. How easy it is to fall a victim of one's own argument.

Politically then we accept that there are many excellent brains bent towards the processes of change and trying to introduce that change. But running a country is like trying to steer an enormous lorry and trying to drive it as if it were a racing car.

There are two special factors to be kept in mind in criticizing a government of a political group. The first is that many of the factors which create instability come from outside the system and are beyond the control of those in charge, and secondly the very difficulty experienced in introducing change is a part of the safeguard against the too complete control that we could have exercised on people—what we have referred to again and again as totalitarianism, in order to give it a simple label; it should perhaps have been called despotism or superfascism.

The point about security in the age of computers and cybernetics is most important. In principle, the development of centralized data on people already allows the possibility of unscrupulous control. Although the use of a civil service and documented data on matters of tax, health, etc., already provides in principle the information that could be misused by a potential central dictator, it is only with the advent of the computer with its high speed and efficiency that we really offer the potential dictator his opportunity for a takeover.

We urgently need protective measures, such as complex coding and cipher devices, and an organization to ensure their proper use. What the people need is the equivalent of a trade union. Each country or state must have a people's party that is not itself political but collectively ensures that the people are not being unreasonably used. The problem of the social balance of power and the problems of dealing with people who are prepared to buy and sell power arise, but they always do in any case. This time the stakes are higher, and the penalty for failure at least the loss of all individual freedom.

It should be emphasized that the political world, unlike the educational world, is not wholly structured in its activities. The extent to which it is not structured is the extent to which no special qualifications are needed and people are free to manoeuvre and set up groups of people working together for some specific purpose and then working again as individuals for some other end. It bears a close resemblance in this respect to the business world, where all the time complex interrelationships are being set up and broken down again in the search for the satisfaction of some particular goal or subgoal.

Part of the difficulty of the complexity of the structure in which politics operates can be gleaned from the fact that a voter has to make up his mind on which of a number of parties to vote for, in terms of some overall estimate of their pros and cons. Whereas the political parties tend to suggest that they have everything to offer and their opponents have absolutely nothing, almost all intelligent voters realize that it is a question of where the balance of advantage lies, but it is also a question of where it lies in a particular context in time. One may be a radical in one's thinking, but one may still find oneself in a position where radicalism can be served by one party or another according to circumstances.

Indeed, in recent years in Britain there has been a continual suggestion that the two main parties are insufficiently different. Perhaps the answer to this should lie in the fact that it does not really matter whether the two political parties have identical views, as long as they still represent two alternative teams who are prepared to implement an acceptable policy. In other words, you could still vote for a collection of people on the grounds that it is a better team than the other team, regardless of whether their principles are different or not.

In the same way, it is easy to see that the way the Houses of Parliament are organized, and this applies particularly perhaps at the moment to the House of Commons, is unwieldy and in many ways illogical and inefficient. Nevertheless, especially bearing in mind our special plea for inefficiency, it is difficult to see how an alternative system could be evolved which was at the same time democratic. The fact that it is difficult to see an alternative, on the other hand, should not mean that we should accept the existing system as something which is fixed and immutable. In general we could argue that change is characteristic of scientific development and therefore we may expect Parliament to change. Our problem will be to try to ensure that the change is of a sensible and useful kind. After all, in Britain, even rugby football and cricket have recently changed their laws and on the whole tended to produce, as a result, a better game. If such conservative games as these can be put into an evolutionary state, it certainly must be the case that our governing system also can.

We are finishing this chapter then on a note of counter-warning. It would be absurd to think that to be scientific is to be right; to be human is to be right, and to understand what this can mean and how it can be achieved to be scientific is a great help.

11 The Emotional World

"People say in Boston
Even beans do it . . ."

Cole Porter

"Do what you will, this world's a fiction
And is made up of contradictions."

William Blake

"In hours of deep emotion, in hours when danger threatens those
we love, we chatter out uneasily the names of invented Gods."

"The Pathetic Fallacy"
Llewellyn Powys

ONE REASON why science, at least in the narrow sense, is in
some disrepute is that it is too often thought of as dealing only
with rational or logical activities, and this has often been the
case. The word "cold" is often used to describe its activities and
its practitioners, who are depicted as dull bespectacled men in
white coats and surrounded by test-tubes. The word 'hot' by
comparison suggests emotion, and is often associated with that
basic and highly emotive activity sex, but more of that anon.

We are talking now of science, or metascience (the science
of science), in a very general way. Science in this broader sense
includes everything, and especially the emotions, and all that
stems from them.

Let us look carefully at the emotions. In our discussions of
cybernetics we have said that we are concentrating on the purely
rational features of the problem of copying humanlike behaviour,
and this is true, not because the emotional side cannot be dealt
with, but because it does not serve a practical purpose, although

133

it is also because the problem is admittedly rather more difficult to deal with.

What exactly are the emotions and how do they operate in human beings and animals? The answer is not completely agreed by scientists at this stage, but we can guess fairly well about their general role, even if we sometimes fail to understand the detail.

Emotional systems seem to have developed much earlier than the rational systems of the brain if we are to judge by the development of the human nervous system. This means that human beings must have needed, for example, in order to survive to react quickly to danger. Indeed it is good "theory of evolution" to argue that only such people (or animals) that can react quickly enough to danger can survive. The emotions therefore are primarily biological systems that encourage the body's activity; they speed up the heart rate and facilitate the flow of blood through the body. This makes it easier for people to use their muscles to good effect, whether they use them to run away or to fight.

But like the operation of any other systems, certain side effects are produced. The increase of heart rate makes people go white in the face, or go red, it makes their hair stand on end, and so on and so forth. These features are incidental to the primary evolutionary function of the emotions. But there are two other incidental although vital aspects of the emotions to be considered. One is that we as human beings have learned to recognize a reddening face or a whitening face as signs of states of emotion, whether of fear or rage. A part of the recognition process naturally depends upon the total context in which the behaviour occurs and this is one reason why we tend to think of emotions less as an internal fuse-box arrangement and more as the external signs of an emotional state.

The other side of this coin is the development of the humanities, as we tend to call them. We must think of these as primitive forms of explanation, as religion and as art, but also as positive motive forces in the form of sex. But we must also look at them as being much more than this, and this is where we find "traditional" science too narrow and lacking in humanity.

In the end, it may be our emotions that are dominant and the principle of hedonism which springs from the emotions is all we are really concerned with. It may be the spiritual world—a world of emotions mixed with reason?—that matters most. But whatever the facts and whatever we must persuade ourselves to believe, we must, it seems, first of all use our dispassionate scientific method to analyse the facts.

As far as cybernetics is concerned, research has been concentrated on the purely rational, because this is, or has been, of most use to man. This is true whether we are thinking of man as a businessman, an educationalist, a politician or even indeed as a scientist. This does not mean that emotions cannot be simulated in an artificial form, it just means that no one has yet tried seriously to do so. There seems to be no "percentage" in doing so.

We may soon try to reproduce genuine computer music and poetry, but the word "genuine" here implies that it must be capable of arousing feelings in the "social being" which is now artificially constructed, the argument still being that, from a scientific point of view, the arts and religion are by-products of a biological system which happened to be necessary for survival.

At this moment in time, we can easily copy the effect of human emotions on rational behaviour, and we can do this by what we call computer simulation. We need though to build a humanlike system by biological means if we are to reproduce humanlike emotions themselves.

Now let us carry out a typical cybernetic strategy and look at the arts, religion and social man, especially in his sexual activity, all as part of the social being that is man, and woman too. First of all we shall look at "the arts".

Taking the name "the arts" in its broadest sense to include writing, music and the pictorial arts, such as painting, sculpture and the like, it is of importance that we should try to trace its past and future development.

Inevitably tracing the future, by our own cybernetic arguments, means examining the past. In examining the past, let us not pretend to great literary depth but attempt to examine and explain the findings in terms that are essentially social, since human beings are above all social beings.

All art is a type of information processing. Poetry has been described as "painting with words", and the tapestries of our times—past, present and future—are made more acceptable by the arts. For some people, the arts have the same role as religion, acting variously as a social cement, as a purpose, a goal, or set of goals, a sort of end-in-itself, or as an escape from the realities, often the grim realities, of existence.

Insofar as the arts are a source of direct and immediate pleasure, their appeal must be to the emotions as well as to the reason, a sort of insight as to people and their motives, their desires and their relationships with each other, indeed all the features of life that are not dealt with by the established sciences—as yet. This is not, of course, the whole story, but it is certainly a part of it. If we wish to know how a person will behave under a certain set of conditions, such as being separated from his wife, or when abroad or in prison, or when his wife has a miscarriage—there are a whole host of such examples—then today we may ask the psychologist, the sociologist or the psychiatrist. But until recently, and for many people even now, we have had to rely on our immediate experience of life.

The obvious difficulty about relying on experience is that it may be too limited and cannot easily be made explicit and handed on from generation to generation. Science can do this, but cannot, as yet, deal realistically with every type of social situation.

One aspect of the arts is, therefore, clearly to help us extend our personal experience; it is in this sense entirely complementary to science. It is not so much that this is what writers, poets and composers set out specifically to do, it is just a fact that they have actually had this effect. It is obviously unnecessary to add that an artist's motives may be far more complicated than this and far from clear in every case even to the artist himself.

We have argued that the arts in one of their principal roles have the problem of extending people's experience. Indeed, take a piece of description which might occur in a novel:

> "Jane was all I had hoped for, and yet I could see the close resemblance to her sister, and this resemblance alone created a difficulty for me . . ."

We must ask if we can yet systematically treat this sort of situation in scientific terms. The answer is as yet 'no'. The novel has exploited special features of information flow and made the most of poetic facility to amplify the informative content of the prose.

We can consider a number of almost classical human situations and analyse them dramatically and poetically through the medium of the novel. Thornton Wilder's novel *Bridge of San Luis Rey* considers what set of occurrences could be responsible for bringing together a group—a rather mixed group—of people to plunge them to their collective death. Coincidence is used in many novels, and no one uses it more than L. P. Hartley. In *The Boat*, for example, the accidental discovery of an important letter is the lynch-pin on which the whole book turns.

Another type of causal sequence is utilized by Rex Warner in his novel *Why Was I Killed?* Here the upright citizen who pleads that he has spent his life working for peace asks why he should be the innocent victim of war. A reflection on the consequences of his actions persuades the reader that while he may have wished for peace, and indeed hated war, he failed to see that his other ambition worked against his desire for peace. In fact, by bringing pressure on the government for higher living standards, even though only for his children and not himself, he was working inconsistently with his peaceful aims. Such examples abound! In more abstract terms, we find novels like Kafka's *The Trial* dealing with the more dreamlike awareness of human beings in their imagination. This imaginative skill allows people to understand and feel things in various ways and various dimensions. The physical fact of dreaming is a reminder that we can transpose and reinterpret all sorts of factual material in a more or less poetic manner. What is interesting is the insight apparently afforded by such new vantage points, within their social context.

Poetry takes full advantage of the levels of consciousness and examines our experience from a variety of different standpoints. With the movement of Auden, Spender, Day Lewis and others in the nineteen-thirties, it became clear that a poet's job was often to deal with people and their half-conscious thoughts and attitudes to a whole range of human activities. They particularly dealt with the social and the political. So much of what is usually called "political" is evocative of the emotions, and hence the food of poets, rather than the powers of reason which are often used to provide the original political analysis.

What then is the real effect of the arts on people? This is strictly a scientific question and the complement of the artistic question as to the significance of science. The answer of the arts is implicit; the answer of the sciences is explicit. Both have their value. The arts have been information processors of the past, and have worked on a broad canvas, including the emotions and the imagination. In fact, this is their special claim, to involve "the whole man". They have been a source of pleasure and dreaming. They have played a role similar to that of religion in creating an aura of security and satisfaction and of understanding for people.

In the course of evolution, their role has obviously changed; this can be seen clearly by even the most casual study of world literature. A part of the reason for this is that the arts represent, quite literally, the process of reflecting the current state of society, the needs and beliefs of the times. There is perhaps no better example of this than in Russian literature, where the geographical conditions play such an important part in the people's lives. The music and the writings of the Scandinavians possess a similar quality of reflecting the moods of those who pass their lives in sombre ways. The Renaissance paintings of Italy with their emphasis on light could never have been painted in Britain, and so the story goes on repeating itself in example after example. Let us now turn to a consideration of some of the religious aspects of our problem.

Human beings, we have repeatedly claimed, are adaptable, but are not sufficiently adaptable to keep abreast of their intellectual and imaginative development, to say nothing of their scientific development. We have agreed further that society has to be rethought to bring it into a more dynamic form where the acceptance of change as well as change itself are built-in features.

Man's suggestibility harnessed to our very powerful scientific "knowhow" is to have the effect of allowing us to free ourselves from our material bondage. The age-old dream of freedom from the limitations of the purely bodily is now certainly possible;

the idea of an emancipated mind or spirit is a reality, but for *totally different reasons* from the ones normally given by the idealists and religionists of the past. The truth is that through being a hundred per cent materialistic in our methods of pursuing knowledge, we can be freed from the bondages of gross materialism. This can be nothing less than ironic: the effect of science on science.

The method of achieving such freedom depends upon the ability to have all the appropriate feelings without the need to transport the physical body through space. In broad terms, the sensations of movement, of seeing new things and having new feelings can be reproduced at home. No one even in 1970 who has psychedelic experiences in the theatre, for example, to say nothing of simpler input systems like cinerama, can doubt the possibility of transporting the experience to the person rather than have the person go to the experience.

This is not to say that all our research in supersonic jet and interstellar rocket flight has been wasted, far from it. The position is that such sensory communication cuts out vast tracks of physical activity that would otherwise have been necessary, or at the very least desirable. We shall always travel in space and time, but the purposes for which we travel will narrow to the point where we say as we sometimes do today "I'll actually *do it* this time, for a change". In fact, we shall almost certainly lose the ability to make this distinction, but this is what will be implied.

The problem which we have recognized and see in embryo now in 1970 is as to the purpose of living; this is a problem for both the arts and religion. Science says it knows nothing of a cosmic purpose. This is natural since we have made the point again and again that we cannot interpret, explain or understand what occurs outside the range of our immediate experience. We have no reason to doubt that the world is in some sense an accident. It could be countered that there is no reason to doubt that there exists a universal purpose, which indeed to some people apparently makes more sense, or is more plausible.

We are now on familiar ground. As scientists we can argue that assuming cosmic purpose is nonsense. We do not, on the assumption of Occam's razor, need to consider such questions at all. In fact, it could be argued that such questions are meaningless since words like 'cause', 'accident' and 'purpose' are a part of our limited experience and indeed have emerged from precisely that same experience. Can we have what we might call universal causes which operate, as it were, outside our system? This is like asking whether time has a beginning and an end, or space has boundaries. Always we are tempted to ask what happened before time began and what will happen after time has stopped. The truth is that in both cases the concepts are part of the system and internal to it and make no sense outside it, since we cannot in material terms get outside.

We turn back to the arts now and assert that we are looking for an answer to a question and the question is as to the nature of what is real, and we remember our language problems and recognize that by 'real' we may mean many different things.

The real world, to the empiricist philosopher and scientist, is described in the language of stick and stones. It is concerned with material objects, and some will argue that this is all there is in the world. It is, they assert, a misunderstanding to ask about so-called spiritual things; these are by-products of the material world. We only have to remember our example of a motor car and its performance to recognize this way of looking at things.

But the arts are not concerned with what is real in this sense. Artists use appearances in the same way as the hard-headed empiricist, but they are not concerned with the explanation of appearances in terms of a consistent internal picture, a picture which improves prediction and increases understanding. Or at least if they are, they are not placing their emphasis on the same purpose.

D. H. Lawrence was concerned with drawing attention to factual ills, but only to set up the same satisfying hymn of discontent of the kind that we hear in the negro spiritual. T. S. Eliot was telling us about our absorption with the most mundane and the trivial aspects of life, and Aldous Huxley's writing served as a permanent reminder of the bitch goddess success. He made the point frequently in his writing of the futility of pursuing material ends. Indeed, in simpler fashion he also pointed out the childishness of pure acquisition, whether in the collector of *objets d'art*—which most of us excuse—or in the case of a Casanova who, as it were, represented each conquest with a swastika, although not in this case stuck on the side of his aircraft.

Auden, Spender and Day Lewis were telling us of our political shackles. Joyce and Virginia Woolf of our intellectual shackles: our loss or lack of imagination. These and a thousand other writers and poets were concerned with our ability to live beyond the immediate material things and although their recipes varied from living as Lawrence would have it, from the very intestines themselves, to Charles Morgan who asked for a civilized appraisal of the "still centre" of things, each and everyone was concerned with providing us with some sort of goal.

It is in the provision of a goal that science differs, *in practice*, from the arts. The pursuit of knowledge is the pursuit of science. This is a search for truth and has a sort of almost unlimited practical payoff; it satisfies all the pragmatic criteria. The search for truth is a way of describing the search of the artist, but now he is in search of a variety of different goals and not just a single one. The artist sees truth pictorially in any incident or fact which is interpreted by his eye and illumined by his skill. The poet is more concerned with his feelings; what is truth for him is the sense of what is worthwhile, but worthwhileness is obviously difficult to define. We are in some difficulty now because we have no clear goal; we do not wish to explain anything, we are not seeing material truth. Although we must retain these points about what our goals are, we must look again for the moment at the more social aspect of the influence of the arts.

Apart from matters of the natural and corporate life, we also have to consider the political and social. So, for example, Ibsen, Bernard Shaw and Sean O'Casey are reminders of how the arts—in this case the theatre—can play a vital role as a critic of society and its trends. This is surely one role they will always play, since in spite of our pleas that more logic and less emotion is needed in our political leaders, such a state can never be wholly achieved, even it it were in any way desirable; for psychological reasons it is, in fact, not desirable as we have already made clear.

What are the psychological factors underlying the arts? Can

we relate such factors to people and their everyday needs? This makes us look at sex with a very much more careful eye.

We have argued that it is survival that is the lynch-pin of our motives, and sex—although certainly very much a primary motive—is in most ways dependent upon survival.

The fact is that we should look at society from two points of view at least, and it can be seen that from a negative point of view survival is everything, but from a positive point of view sex, hunger, thirst and the other primary motivators are the most vital ones. It is to this extent, no doubt, that the psycho-analysts are correct and sex is absolutely basic.

The facts of sex have been systematically dealt with in the Kinsey Report, among other places, and we need not repeat or attempt to amplify these reports. Perhaps the most significant feature of most "professional" books on sex, books which purport to advise people on what they should do, how often they should do it and also what they should feel, is the basic defect of most books which purport to instruct people. The fact is that the range of individual differences and their needs is far greater than is normally admitted. There is considerable evidence that the nature of the orgasm varies considerably from person to person, and everyone knows that for the same person it varies from time to time.

What is less well known is that the nature of sexual expression takes a variety of forms which are all "normal" to the people expressing them. Obviously homosexuality is "normal" to those people who, as a result of a particular glandular state, coupled with particular life experiences, have only homosexual interests.

Sex is basic to survival as far as the species is concerned, since if sex were not practised it is fairly obvious that civilization would die out. This is one quite practical explanation of why homosexuality is regarded as immoral. It is a threat to survival, and this is the basis of much, if not all, of morality. This shows man in his vital social role.

One of the habits of peoples is to build moral codes around basic human motives. It is for this reason that sex in the western world is made sacrosanct as between two people of the opposite sex. Morality immediately says that such a pair should remain together and remain constant to each other. Of course, not all societies have taken the same view and one feature of this variation is to ask ourselves whether or not the religious-based morality reflects what is either God-given or good sense.

At this point, as far as Christian society is concerned, the family unit comes into the limelight. Is it, as it is sometimes claimed, the "natural" unit?

This sort of question can be answered in various ways. It seems certain that the family unit is not "natural" in the sense of being the only way of providing for survival of children. It is, however, convenient in many ways (and for many of us highly desirable) and one we have become used to, at least certainly in the western world. For some people it is ideal, but for many it is very unsatisfactory. The divorce rate, which steadily climbs year by year, is an indication of the need for easier transfer from partner to partner, but this mitigates against the ideal background in which to nurture children. One solution is therefore to place all children under state care from the start.

This last suggestion characteristically evokes a great deal of emotion, which is understandable in terms of the artistic and religious views of the world. What is required by them is something emotionally, aesthetically and romantically satisfying. Perhaps 'romantic' is too "soft" a term to describe an attitude which can often be quite Spartan and may become almost infinitely dedicated.

Does science offer any alternative to this almost traditionally accepted western social view? The answer here must be "yes", if only because our whole thesis hinges on the adaptability and conditionability of human beings. Whereas they cannot always change quickly enough to meet the demands of changing circumstances, at least it is known that with time and under extreme pressures adaptability can be extremely rapid. This is one more reason to fear a rising totalitarianism which can be accepted so easily under conditions of stress. In other words, our ability to adapt to the wrong thing is as great, or almost so, as our ability to adapt to the right thing.

The question of accepting state ownership of children hinges on the needs of society as a whole. If we avoid revolution, but still arrive at a totalitarian state, and a revolution itself is in any case bound to lead there, then we can be sure of the strongest vested interest in the direct control of the community's children. To have them all from birth, or nearly so, under state surveillance is merely playing into the hands of those who wish for a perpetual and self-improving control.

The answer in turn to this lies in what we ourselves are hoping to achieve. Copulation stands independent of the production of children. With appropriate contraceptive methods, sexual intercourse becomes socially far less important. To have sexual intercourse could become no more significant than having a drink or taking one of the milder forms of drug.

Parents might in such a state have to be paid to have children. The more instinctive need to procreate could itself be offset by appropriate chemical control.

Here, as so often, we see science as the key to the control of our environment. At any given time, we may say that this or that cannot be done because we do not *yet* know how to do it, but in most cases we can guess that the time will come when we shall know how.

The degree of understanding that allows us to evolve socially in a controlled way is at the same time an advantage and a threat. We can make our machines evolve far faster than we can evolve ourselves, so we are threatened by their building, and it is because of this that we shall almost certainly build the inevitable "superspecies"; what is so vital is whether we can learn to control it, or at least retain its favours.

All the time we can control our own destiny, we should try to decide what it is that we want to achieve. We must, as we have said repeatedly, never talk of "ultimate goals", since there is no reason to suppose an "ultimate state" for man, unless, of course, it is final oblivion. So it is that we must seek merely to assess the goal of the next phase and perhaps guess at the one after that. Without such assessing of goals, we can make no sense of our present activity. This is good "cybernetic thinking".

What then are we to say about the complete separation of sexual satisfaction from family life? What we probably will say is "keep the family", but what will gradually happen is the decay of the family as a unit, and its replacement by more transient sexual relationships without family responsibilities. What then will be the outcome?

In answering the last question, we are placed in much the same position as in answering the question about the effect of automation on society. We relieve ourselves of work and produce the very boredom we most wish to avoid. In depriving ourselves of the responsibilities for bringing up children we destroy one of the most potent factors in education. We learn a sense of proportion and we learn about ourselves and about life by raising a family, and its absence is one further factor which could create the sort of sterility for which we are heading.

At this stage we must warn ourselves again that we shall at least partially evolve and adapt to these changes, so that what at first sight seems to be a stupid and futile type of development may, for the society which adopts it, merely seem normal. But having said that, we have to face the fact that the very adaptation process itself is capable of being directed and we are still left with the need to decide which way we need to direct affairs.

As we have mentioned, psychoanalysts tend to interpret all human behaviour in terms of sexual activity, but we would prefer to argue that in the motivational hierarchy it is survival that is the fundamental feature. There are also many other primary drives, which include sex, as well as hunger, thirst, etc., which are basic conditions of survival for the organism. Security is such a large psychological factor in everyone's welfare that it must reflect the basic importance of survival.

How then do the arts and religion fit into this scheme of things? The answer is that they originally fitted in because they supplied precisely the information needed to understand and predict the environment. They were playing, in other words, precisely the role that science is now taking over.

Over and above that, the emotional appeal of the artistic and religious method created additional satisfaction, akin to that of the debater whose eloquence is more effective than his logic. Life is lived by human beings and cannot be lived adequately on the purely rational plane. One problem is that for so much of one's life a person can feel depressed or elated without relation, or without obvious relation, to the empirical facts.

Literature and poetry have dealt extensively with the "halcyon days", especially those of childhood; they also deal with the memories, the sunlight, the ecstacy and the remembered sadness. The story is one mainly of youth and of hope.

There is something indeed to be said for the idea that most of what literature and poetry are about is birth and death. Copulation and social motives come in between and the only real tragedy is that of getting old. These are the factors which inspire emotion, and often provide people with a sense of worthwhileness which transcends all other features of their immediate environment. Literature and poetry can have the effect of making you think *and feel* that there is nothing other than the transcendental dream which creates an overwhelming feeling of wellbeing and satisfaction, and this is where art merges with religion.

What, though, does this all mean when interpreted scientifically? Are artistic and religious experiences the same? Whether they are or not, is there any systematic way that such satisfactions can be maintained and made regularly available?

This last consideration raises the whole problem of such uncertain fields as hypnosis and extrasensory perception and the certain fields of drugs, such as lysergic acid, which heighten one's perception and one's imagination and provide a key to the route to the control of the imagination.

From the start of this book we have realized the possibility of pushing away from the bodily and the material towards the 'mental', for want of a better word—some may prefer the word 'spiritual'. Whatever the resolution of the semantic problem, it seems clear that we can greatly extend the power of suggestion. The existence of primitive religious conversion is but one example of the power to persuade people against their ordinary rational convictions.

A number of experiments have been done on people kept in isolation, and in one particular experiment, carried out in Canada, in which the present author participated, people were kept in complete isolation even to the extent of being blindfolded, handcuffed—in effect—and kept in an airconditioned box for as long as a week at a time. They had earphones on and could hear only what was said to them over the "intercom".

The results of these experiments were, to say the least, dramatic. It was clear that even relatively bad propaganda was effective in producing real changes of attitude, and states of great emotion. Many subjects, so treated, claimed with great conviction that their food was being poisoned and that they were in other ways being persecuted. There was certainly no truth in these allegations.

Brainwashing is the process of changing people's views and making them think what you want them to, more or less irrespective of the facts. That this can be achieved is undoubted; what is much more relevant is the fact that this will also be possible with much greater ease in the future; a mere pill may provide all that is necessary. In a mild way the arts provide such stimulation, but the mildness refers only to the definiteness of the effects. The effects when they occur for certain individuals can be dramatically satisfying, as we have already said, and most of us have directly experienced them.

To date, the arts have been built around sights, sounds and the imagination. The psychedelic approach of Marshall McLuhan can drastically change this situation and provide a new world of the imagination; a world which would, in some measure, replace the world of empirical facts which, for the majority, is heading directly towards boredom, and hence totalitarianism or extinction, or both.

The question of our proper (short-term) goal now looms up once more. If we clarify our goal and keep away from material prediction, then we move across that ill-defined boundary from the arts to religion. We are again in a special situation and the question is as to what we want, or perhaps what we need. Voltaire's comment that "man made God in his own image" is most relevant. We would say that if God did not exist we should have to invent him, because of the need for some "supergoal".

The word 'God' is itself extremely difficult to define and we can, of course, mean a variety of different things by it. The scientist reacts often adversely to statements such as "God is a person", or "There exists a personal God" or "God is the father". All these statements are manifestly a generalization from our immediate experience and are cast, perhaps inevitably, in crude material terms. In fact, if our guide to any future religion lies in the past then we are in a hopeless plight since science has shown that most religions are based on primitive explanations of the universe.

We have said it before, that when Mr. Oxlee has been drowned at sea, it is because the revengeful spirit of his mother-in-law has proved too powerful. In the *Iliad* too we find Hector asking for help from his Gods when pursued by Achilles around the walls of Troy. The whole of Greek mythology is filled with the interferences of the Gods to protect their earthly comrades. This is the use of an anthropomorphic explanatory principle operating in reverse. There is, as a result, no further need for material explanation.

In future religion will look very different. One possibility is that Christianity as we know it today will still be in existence but will become less and less effective. In saying this we have to add the point that we do not, or should not, think of Christianity as an integrated and clearcut philosophy or religion. Far from it; rather like socialism and many other 'isms, there are almost as many versions of Christianity as there are people. Nor is this necessarily a bad thing, since those religions which have almost fossilized their views and been most autocratic in their organization and control of their flock are those that most need help to adapt.

The Roman Catholic church—among the Christian sects—is the obvious target we have in mind. Its strength and its weakness both stem from its inflexibility. To be in the Vatican City is to be greatly impressed by the grandeur of the architecture, by the beauty of the surroundings, but also by the commercial nature, as well as the spiritual nature, of the whole undertaking. Many Roman Catholic cathedrals exhibit the same unabashed commercialism which to some of us seems downright cynical.

The whole development of Catholicism is an attempt to be both realistic and autocratic at the same time. This is the most successful Christian *qua* Christian approach to date, but must ultimately fail because of science and scientific method. It is not what Catholics say or even do, most of the time, but their uncritical commitment to absolute and arbitrary standards that makes it a religion that must be self-destroying unless, of course, it provides the fascist seeds which we have continually claimed are being sown.

The Protestant Church fails because, while it accepts science and adapts to it, it has lost as a result the very arbitrary source of faith which makes a religion possible, and is indeed its very heart and being.

We can and must supply a recipe which will probably prove in time to be acceptable to both Christian and humanist, and indeed to all people in the universe at the next phase of development.

In the end, people are practical; an idea which is a bad one is thrown out and a good one is retained. If this ceased to be so, civilization itself would cease to exist. Our problem is, though, that it is getting too difficult to tell whether an idea is good or bad, in this specialist age of science.

There is no point in dividing the motivations, the needs and the general forces of life over trivialities like contraceptives, the evidence of miracles, the sectarian differences between Christians. Everyone, or almost everyone, knows this to be absurd. But the reason we cannot say so too often, if at all, is because we might in the process shatter the gossamer with which the necessary magic is weaved.

We can liken the position to that of a prime minister, say, in 1970. He cannot publicly say "Ignore Mr. X since he is a thoroughly unpleasant man (not his actual phrase) and is complaining almost entirely because I did not offer him a post in the Government". If he says this, Mr. X only denies it and says "The Prime Minister must go because he is incompetent and I have never wished to serve in his or any other government". The Prime Minister now fumes with anger but cannot say "But what about that conversation after the dinner at Y. You made it absolutely clear to me . . .". The truth is useless, or rather it is unusable. You do not know nor can you know who is telling the truth and who is lying, or what percentage of either is being done by whom.

So we must not destroy that delicate fabric of uncertainty on which our imagination feeds. We can and will be more emphatic than this. We will say that the needs of the people must be served and these needs are *not* necessarily served by truth. We remind ourselves at this point that we cannot know the actual state and origin of the universe, so that sort of truth is not in any case involved.

We are concerned with the pragmatic—the practical—truth;

what is *useful* is true. This is the basis for interpreting God, not discussing whether God exists or not. This is *not* a cynical undertaking, but more nearly an artistic one. We are saying that God is whatever is the integrating factor, the organizational power behind appearances. There is an organization, even if some people see the world as disorganized, and that organization *is* God. We may wonder whether there is more than a tangential relationship between this concept we are suggesting and many people's current views of God as a loving universal parent, a universal information source or intergalactic computer. But such discrepancies are not necessarily relevant; the difficulty is to allow our imagination to rise to new heights. We shall try to do just this.

Our fabric is a speculative account of reality and we suggest that we can first describe that reality in the following terms. We shall speak first as an atheist and say that the universe has existed from all eternity and the change of state which allowed life to emerge from non-living systems was fortuitous in the sense that it was not the focal point of a purpose and certainly did not involve any person; the idea of a sort of superfather who created man and gave him freewill is fatuous. The whole idea of a personal loving God and the story of Jesus and his rising from the dead are a mere projection of our wishes. Religion represents a sort of wish-fulfilment and cannot be supported by any evidence whatever. It is, as Freud has said, an illusion and one that we may or may not wish to nurture but has in any case no truth behind it. A person holding such a view as we are describing might add that much of what most Christians say is virtually meaningless and for the rest there is no way of knowing whether it is true or not. There is, however, much evidence from anthropology and psychology to account for religious views, Christian or otherwise, without for a moment believing them to be correct.

To take one example of the problems of meaning, we must say what we mean by the word 'God'. What indeed do we mean by 'God'?

At this stage we shall say that if you accept the framework of evidence and explanation set up by us in the context of scientific method, then it would be difficult to find fault with the above argument. Even within this context, though, a Christian might still argue that there was historical evidence in the life and death of Jesus that supported a belief in the existence of God. There may be other debatable points that could be raised, but by and large the Christian would rely, and should rely, on faith and the claim of personal experience, and most important of all, would point out that it was *not* explanation he was interested in. He would begin from personal experience, so that the question of the existence of God would be by no means a starting point.

If you are seeking explanations in the scientific sense, you can give no complete explanation of God, his purposes and the history and origin of life. Nor can anyone else? The scientist–agnostic would accept this but could claim to have some hope that we would in time be able to explain the origins of life. There is even in 1970 a great deal of the most pertinent evidence available.

We now run into another problem. Many Christians and other religionists will argue that it is not wholly a matter of faith to believe in God. Faith for them represents rather one jump in an otherwise logical picture that may be incomplete but is not illogical.

If we now take an extreme Christian view, we shall say that the Bible is our authority as the word of God provides literal explanations of historical matters. We shall not pursue this point of view, merely note that some part of this argument is testable and some part depends directly, as to its testability, on the meaning we ascribe to the word 'God'.

We have, as can easily be seen, provided enough information to make it clear that complete confusion could easily ensue in any discussion of religion. The domain in which such arguments could be couched by a less "fundamental" type of Christian view could be very much more abstract. God is what guides the world, a force of some sort, envisaged as a person and essentially personal in "his"—we have to say it—love and personal care for us.

Naturally a hopeless morass of confusion can be built up around subjects like miracles, the nature of the Trinity, the virgin birth and other theological matters, whether treated as literal or metaphorical. So where is all this leading?

F

We are suggesting that a prescription is possible which will become more or less acceptable to all points of view, and we can see now what this prescription will be. Let us try to hint at it.

We do not believe in God, if by God you mean a person like a human or superhuman being who occupies space and time. More briefly, the humanist may say "I do not believe in God". From now on we shall speak of humanist and Christian as the two main viewpoints under consideration, bearing in mind that the words 'humanist' and 'Christian' are being used here only as rough labels. To make a success of the argument we need both parties to be sophisticated and understanding and with a common desire to join forces.

The Christian will say "I do believe in God, but I do not know the nature of God, and cannot; I conceive of "Him" by necessity—or certainly by convenience and also be faith—as personal. By personal I mean benevolent." We shall not press him for evidence for existence because my humanist friend is right in saying that from his point of view God does not exist. We are not seeking evidence about a material thing, because what we conceive of as Godlike is no more material than the performance of my automobile.

The humanist could question the use of the word 'material', but knowing that semantics will not serve anyone much here and since he is now actively trying to help the discussion, he merely asks how the performance is shown in the world. The answer must be in human beings especially, but in all things that exist, since by 'God' I mean in a sense all that is, or rather the performance of all that is.

Some Christians will wish to dress their beliefs in the formal concepts and phrases of the Bible, but fundamentalism itself must vanish. By 2000, no one except the most primitive people could seriously believe in a 'fundamentalist'—if one may borrow the word here—humanist view. Young people particularly may not have the need from which God springs.

"If a God does not exist, we must invent him." Many people have made this observation in one way or another, even apart from Voltaire. Can we make the invention a discovery? The answer lies in the imagination, the consciousness and the abstract ability of man. It also depends on our ability to be flexible and see the same things—the same patterns—in various different ways. This is one of "the problems of various viewpoints" which we mentioned right at the beginning of this book.

We do not talk of creation, but of change; we explain in the material mode and feel love and affection in the non-material mode. That we can explain our behaviour in the non-material mode in terms of the material mode remains a strong possibility. But explaining it is not necessarily changing and certainly not eliminating it. If our imagination is shown to depend upon collections of nerve cells in our brain, it remains the imagination just the same for all that.

When we feel love and ecstasy, and the need for affection, when we express ourselves in poetic terms and have feelings of great depth and emotion, we are not concerned with explanation but with sharpening our feelings and making ourselves even more aware, more flexible and more responsive. This coupled to the sense of wonder at life and its beauty as well as its complexity is what we may call 'worship', and prayer becomes a more specialized form of worship.

Different people have different needs which have to be satisfied by different means. Science will tell us what these are and how to satisfy them. It is science that will make it clear that religion is necessary. But what we mean by religion will vary according to the person you are. By some the same sense of the miraculous and the magic of the world will be said to be natural and essentially non-religious; yet the same feelings and the same responses will be involved.

All this may seem the worst sort of nonsense viewed from the material explanatory mode, and viewed from the religious point of view it may seem absurdly abstract. It is nevertheless the best we can do in applying language descriptively to attitudes and feelings, thoughts and ambitions, which are essentially organic and are an integral part of ourselves.

We shall gradually evolve to this new sort of attitude by the year 2000, and by then much of the source of argument between Christian and humanist will seem childlike. The progress, and this seems to be genuine progress, must and will come from the gradual erosion of the outward images, the rituals, often child-like, of the present too literal versions of Christianity. In 1970,

F*

what all too many preachers in church and chapel say is more infantile and meaningless—both in feeling and informatory content—than the conversation of young children. What the formal Church has obscured is the reality of God, dressing "Him" as they do into a kinglike puppet.

The passing from communication by language to direct sensory communication will provide the evolutionary step needed to bring about a religion, or philosophy, which could be worldwide and itself in evolution; it could and will cater for the everyday needs of people.

The reconstruction of the past and the destruction, by our efficient coding systems and data banks, of the sense of passing time is the reason we shall need less by way of a personal God in the future, and more by way of an abstract plan and a guardian of the universe.

In discussing universities in an earlier chapter, we saw that they were the cradle for new ideas, new concepts, whose very job, therefore, made them guardians of our social freedom. They are often the people least interested in religion and most interested in a more emphatic humanism. They provide a feedback in our society which adjusts society to a road which may itself be provided by the abstract thinking of the older generation.

Society is cybernetic and we expect and need continual adjustments to our goal-seeking activity. The examination of both means and ends is a function for the whole of society and one that by 2000 will be participated in by the whole of society. To this end our universal system will be, as we have already argued, thoroughly overhauled and brought into line with the needs of the times. This in turn acts as a feedback to the schools and the rest of our educational system, and then the whole thing treads the tightrope between inefficiency and injustice in pursuit of the ideas which we have argued are the same in essence whether you think of yourself as a man of letters, poet, fundamentalist, Christian or an atheist.

The emotional world can be explained, and can also be changed, but remains one of our mainsprings; it is what makes us human beings, and it can perhaps be used to humanize our new machine species.

12 Society: AD 2000 and Beyond

"What candles may be held to speed them all?
Not in the hands of boys, but in their eyes
Shall shine the holy glimmers of goodbyes."

"Anthem for Doomed Youth"
Wilfred Owen

"—— Now I want
Spirits to enforce, art to enchant
And my ending is despair,
Unless I be relieved by prayer;
Which pierces so that it assaults
Mercy itself and frees all faults
As you from crimes would pardon'd be
Let your indulgence set me free."

"The Tempest"
William Shakespeare

IN THIS LAST chapter, we shall try to look a little further into the future, as well as draw together the arguments that have formed the threads of the whole book. We shall talk briefly of the state of affairs likely to exist at the end of the century, and hint at least at the further future.

Social attitudes and standards are changing fast; religion and the changing face of philosophy is a reality in the western world, and we find it increasingly difficult to discover bedrock, or even anything that might serve as bedrock. The old idea of religion or philosophy as a comprehensive source of knowledge or analysis of knowledge has been replaced increasingly by specialist science, analytical thinking and linguistic analysis, and all that this implies. This has had the effect of removing religion and philosophy more and more from everyday life and everyday problems, and concentrating the professional attention of theologians and philosophers on highly academic and often very remote problems.

The increase in the sheer bulk of knowledge, or what has been called the information explosion, has had the most dramatic effect on our lives. It has created specialization and super-specialization, compartmentalizing of knowledge and all the vastly increased problems of communication and control. This is all quite inevitable; what was once easily run as a school, a university, a business or a government becomes infinitely more difficult to develop and control.

It is the great increase in complexity which has bred industrial and management cybernetics. Here we have the capacity to exercise control through cybernetic means which would other-wise have been quite impossible. This means the development of use of software techniques, of more complex machinery, computers, and methods of communication which will, by the end of the century, far exceed anything we have seen so far. But where is all this leading? This is what we have discussed in terms of probable trends and principles, but we are still in need of clarification of these trends and the goals we can accept, and we need above all to be clear about what we need to do in order to achieve our goals, once they have been decided.

Science is developing at an ever-increasing pace, so the role of the businessman, the politician, the academic and the philo-sopher or religionist must change too. This is not to say that economics, politics, philosophy or religion of the existing kind will vanish, but that they will change beyond all recognition and become unrecognizable as a particular part of more general themes; it will be a part of a new and overriding science of science, science of philosophy or philosophy of science or indeed science of systems. Cybernetics, which is the meeting place of all these concepts, will become all-important. It is to be anticipated that this new all-embracing science of science will play a vital role in integrating our total development, and help to apply cybernetics and "total" scientific ideas to all aspects of society. It is an urgent matter that we see the need for such changes, and thus help to try to control our destiny. The inevitable and vast increase in scientific specialization increases the difficulty for the specialist scientist in seeing the effect of his work on the broader social issues, hence the need for greater integration, and perhaps with increased threats from the dangers inherent in too much centralized control. The "total" science we are discussing is total in the sense that it deals with all aspects of our needs and behaviour; it is the *means* par excellence.

We must remember that we have, in the last thirty years, learned more about technology than in the whole history of the human race. We do not need to say that the next thirty years will see the most dramatic changes ever witnessed. It is absolutely essential that we streamline our educational system and make it more flexible. We must undertake the education of people of all ages, and by introducing areas of undercontrol or controlled inefficiency prepare us all for changes which might otherwise topple human society altogether.

As with schools, the job may best be achieved by active participation in society. But this has to be achieved by leading and not driving, and this implies the need to prepare people by a complete statement of ends and means and what the whole process entails.

Next we have the computers and automation which have a direct bearing on our overall science of systems; they are already revolutionizing every aspect of our life. In the short term we see their effect in automation, and the replacement particularly of the unskilled worker. Later we shall see the replacement of the highly skilled worker as well, and thus provide a very much more efficient mode of operation for all our industry and commerce. To such an extent is this likely to take place that the so-called human operator will find no market for his wares.

There is little imagination needed to foresee that we shall control all air traffic and ground traffic by computers within the next ten years.

All information, including the legal and medical, for example, will certainly be completely automated. Decision-taking and conversation with a new computer species is inevitable. All newspapers and all sources of information will be automated, and such other things as medical diagnosis and every kind of robot service will be available to serve human needs.

This in turn will breed a universal language, not Esperanto, but something between a computer language such as COBOL and, say, ordinary English. The compromise necessary as far as language is concerned seems both typical and essential. The idea is that the computer is to be adaptive and to be capable of learning the meaning of new words and adding new words to its vocabulary. All of this is a part of the new man–machine evolution.

There is absolutely no social danger in a language-learning system in isolation. The danger occurs when the system has the range of human experience and is capable of becoming a separate autonomous individual.

The most dangerous example of autonomous individuals lies in the use of "intelligent" robots to do more than routine jobs, rather to have them play the part of military men or policemen or have them carry out the decision-making capacity. All this will happen by 2000, and the implications are almost beyond our ability to predict.

One thing we can predict, however, and that is the need for safeguards to maintain a social balance of power. Trade unions have maintained the balance of power in business and industry, the fact of a political opposition has maintained it in government, and alliances have maintained it internationally. Maintenance of a balance of power is not always easy, and sometimes fails. It is rather like a system seeking a stable state: the difficulty is not so much that of finding it, but of maintaining it once it has been found.

Trade unions are losing their power and the other social balances can be upset all too easily. To maintain a balance usually requires a bargaining power. What power of bargaining will the ordinary individual have in the future in a country that is already overcontrolled?

It has been said by Neville Cardus that the cricket county captains of today are like Pavlov's dogs; they lack imagination and colour. There are no characters left. Much the same seems to be true of baseball, although less so. But the departure of Ted Williams removed one of the last great characters of the game, and those that remain increasingly comply with the controllers in a more and more subservient way.

The other pressing need, apart from finding a new individuality, and mechanism for social safeguards for individual liberty, is that of finding mechanisms for controlling our artificially intelligent systems.

We control human beings by their social sense and their emotions. Perhaps the safety mechanism in robots should be the inclusion of a conscience, but the care with which it should be programmed is fairly clear. We certainly want a sense of very complicated fail-safe mechanisms and this could be a major scientific problem.

The need for privacy and liberty is already recognized in data processing, and laws are being formulated to protect the individual. It should, though, be clearly understood that it is very difficult to achieve such privacy. We know from our wartime efforts how easy it is to break any code that is usable. Some of the great crimes of the future will be in the field of data processing. "Cooking the books" is manifestly easier on the computer than it ever was with the quill pen, and some outstanding crimes along such lines have already been committed. One wonders inevitably how many more have occurred that have not yet been discovered.

The safeguards will, in the future, need to be made much more sophisticated than any we have now. We are only, at this moment, scratching at the surface of the problem. Awareness of the problem and its dramatic dangers is, however, halfway to solving it, and solve it we must if we are to survive.

All these features taken together have dramatic implications for the future of society, even though the precise details of what they will lead to depend in part on the decisions which have to be made in the future by people in the form of governments and so on. These decisions, as yet unknown, will certainly affect the future states of society that we shall achieve. Our object is to ask ourselves what sort of society we need to achieve or need to try to achieve in the light of these inevitable scientific discoveries.

Let us be clear that unless we streamline our educational system along the lines already discussed and streamline our business life, as well as our governmental methods, then our chances of survival are still very poor indeed. Any country or group of countries that does so automatically increases its chances of the things that seem to matter to it—happiness and freedom, without boredom, which could destroy us by making us lazy and by removing all motivation. We are, in effect, in the same danger as the Romans, of hiring mercenaries—this time, machine mercenaries—to do our work for us.

By 'streamline' in the above paragraph, we must be absolutely clear that we do not mean a juggernaut efficiency or conformity or centralized rigid plan. We do mean the taking of every advantage of scientific advances to improve our communication and our understanding and also to make people more "human", although we must decide what we mean here by 'human'. We want controlled inefficiency, or efficient lack of control. The truth is that you must find where and when to leave people alone, and encourage them to become individuals again. The price of this must mean some injustice, but the alternative price is total injustice and extinction.

We fear that our machines will lead us like Rome, and others in turn, into a decline and fall, and it is only through great individuality and by being provided with new worlds to conquer —both intellectual and physical—that we can avoid such a disaster. We have to learn to control our own evolution.

Let us be quite clear that we can never say that we do not want any part of this new life and simply follow the recipe of Rousseau or Lawrence and "go back to nature", because this is impossible. We have to evolve with scientific evolution, and our aim must be to try to see how to control it to achieve what seems to be a satisfactory state of society for the majority, or follow some such principle, even for the short term. This very idea of a "satisfactory state for the majority" is one which one might question, but it is one we can use as a rough guide to the sort of goal we ought to be setting ourselves in the immediate future.

We know that prediction is difficult and we have been talking in terms of a limited aspect of scientific development. At the same time we cannot look too far ahead since prediction over too lengthy a period becomes completely pointless; if we mention "two million years", for example, the thought of predicting is fascinating, but it is in fact, as an undertaking, totally absurd.

In discussing the changing face of society, we are of course absolutely clear that society is changing all the time. We talk about periods of transition, but all we can really say sensibly is that some periods seem to have greater change attached to them than others. Indeed, the effect of science is greatly to increase the rate of change overall for most of us in all aspects of life and in all countries of the world. This is indeed, if you like, a period of transition; the only thing is it is not likely to stop, because the periods of transition are going to become greater and greater. In fact, as we have made clear, transition is life.

We may expect, and this is the obvious short-term effect of automation which is one of our main themes, that the effectiveness of our production will be greatly increased and we shall gradually bring down the working hours of people, and indeed destroy for most people the distinction we now make between work and leisure. To be more specific, we could agree that the introduction of the computer into an industry does not immediately have the effect of reducing the number of people employed; on the contrary, it often increases them in the short term, but at the same time greatly increases their overall efficiency. If it does not increase their overall efficiency it is usually due to the complete mishandling of the computer installation or lack of proper appreciation of its possibilities. That it *can* always increase the efficiency of a system goes without saying, otherwise it should not have been installed in the first place. In the end, however, the effect is inevitably to destroy the need for people themselves, since the computer can become completely self-controlling.

Generally speaking, therefore, our problems in the short term are likely to be problems of finding the appropriate people for the appropriate job, and this means giving people a flexible education as they have to face the possibility of continual re-education throughout the course of their entire working lives. The implications for the educational system are, of course, tremendous and we have already made clear the need for schools and universities along entirely new lines in order to serve people for the whole of their lives.

In the short term, considerable economic problems arise from our need to find markets for our increased production, but in the long term the matter becomes purely one of efficient production distribution. In the field of international competition we have, in the West, to become more closely amalgamated into a bigger bloc, and this is simply one of the steps towards "one world". The immediate alternative to a United States of Europe seems to be to become a sort of additional state to the United States of America, which although probably quite a satisfactory form of solution, seems to be less satisfactory on the whole than becoming the United States of Europe. USE and USA can then merge as a next phase of world integration. The reasons that we must become part of a larger bloc are obvious; the larger-scale the organization of industry and commerce, in general, the more effectively that industry can compete in world markets. Industrial efficiency, by and large, in the world of the computer and automation, tends to be more efficient than the larger bloc on which it is organized.

In the immediate future we may expect great changes in our way of life, a great increase in standardization, which demands the compensation of an increase of individual activity outside the decreasing number of working hours. This means an increase in leisure; it could mean an increase in individual activities directed towards the arts, hence the importance of our discussions on both sex and art, as well as religion, as prominent ingredients of the crucially important "world of emotions".

The question of religion and social motivation is central to our theme, and we have tried to deal with these matters, however briefly; it is all a part of the provision of goals, as opposed to means which are primarily supplied by science. We have the same problems of motivation and leisure activity, standardization and the like rearing their heads in a form which becomes increasingly acute as we pass the point where we need to increase the number of working people to achieve the high degree of efficient automation that we shall achieve in the very near future. Therefore in the longer-term future, and I take this to be something like 20 to 40 years away, we shall find ourselves with a greatly increased, or even totally, leisured population. There will be a completely different ratio of workers in the field, most workers being scientists, medical people, sociologists and the like, who are bound to bring all these same problems of social organization, emotions and motivation to a head.

We must evolve through the period when travel in minutes, by rocket, takes us to any part of our galaxy and even other galaxies, to the point where no travelling, or at least a minimum of travelling, is necessary. If feelings and thoughts can be communicated then the mere body itself can stay at home. This in turn makes clear the fact that men will not leave their homes to "work", only for pleasure and ultimately perhaps not even for that.

With increased climatic control, the question of where one lives—even on what planet—becomes ultimately irrelevant. We accept the fact that people will still be motivated to survive, otherwise that will be the end of human civilization. Indeed, one of our problems is as human beings, that unless we do have problems, difficulties, obstacles to overcome, there is a danger that we shall lose the very motivating factors which are so essential to our survival. Put another way, there is a definite possibility that we shall cease to survive as a species precisely because we have reached the point of inertia, where we need to do nothing but exist. Under these circumstances, individual people become degenerate and as a result extinct, but even as an entire species we might cease to survive. Whether or not, in the end, we would cease to survive as a species is less relevant than the *short-term question* as to what we can do to alleviate the chronic boredom which is obviously going to be our biggest alternative enemy.

We have already laboured the alternative to a failing motivation and that lies in constructing our own superiors, precisely because we can more easily reconstruct our own betters than we can directly improve ourselves. This may be the right choice, but if taken then the whole of our problem becomes one of controlling such a species, by whatever means are possible. It is much the same problem facing a parent who may well breed an offspring far more intelligent than himself.

An alternative possibility is that a sudden breakthrough in communication could allow us to plug one person's nervous system into another's and gradually set up a huge communal brain; this could have the effect of curtailing the development of our rival machine species, or at least providing a control for it. But on the whole the odds are that the machine development will come first and spoil such a possibility, although even a communal brain has its own problems, which could turn out to be worse than the evolution of our machine species.

At the same time we must not overlook the possibility of taking our own mental control and our mental capacity to something far above anything we have achieved so far.

Certainly up to now one can see that human beings have had such a range of problems to interest, stimulate and activate them that the question of becoming bored through lack of stimulation is unthinkable, and it is in this direction that we shall see the most dramatic change. Medicine provides enough problems to keep the whole of the human race busy for many years hence, and activities like it—including the colonization of space—will postpone the inevitable day when *there is nothing for us to do*.

Our coming standardized and automated society provides the problem of education for the leisure which automation supplies in acute form. Therefore we will say again that our educational system is the critical point of departure for the attempted solution for the whole of our problems in the future.

We have suggested that one of the basic motivating factors that could be effective in our expanding universe is the colonization of space. Briefly speaking, the colonization of space would be an exact copy of the previous colonization of the surface of the earth. This would provide precisely the right sort of stimulating and adventurous environment in which human beings could keep or retain enough fortitude for the battle of human survival. Be this as it may, the use of drugs and pharmacological aids is bound to play an increasingly important part in civilization. The current role of alcohol and drugs is a motivational stimulant which cannot be ignored and plays an increasing part in the alleviation of our current problem.

The undoubted decay of religious influence and the loss of the "social cement" that religion supplied has left a gap in our sociological armament. This could be refilled by a new religion and this is a further real alternative; its conception and implementation could be the most important thing in the whole history of civilization. This is undoubtedly a problem for the sociologist to study and indeed is one of the reasons why we expect to see a large development in the social sciences. But in the meantime one has to face the fact that increased leisure implies increased time for rumination about the nature of reality and the nature of "being" and raises problems over existing religions. These problems occur because of the belief that there is no truth in the essential ontological claims of existing religion. This could indeed lead to widespread depression and pessimism, and gain increased use or need for drugs and other stimulants. But the alternative may lie in the dangerous process of throwing out truth as we have usually thought of it.

It is not enough to look to the behaviouristically conditioned future, and say, leaning heavily on Shakespeare, that this is "death to the individuality and spirit which is essential to humanity", as well as at the same time utterly overlooking the fact that no external critic could have evolved to such a state. All we are trying to do is predict and understand so that we can plan ahead.

The chances are that by 2000 we shall already be unrecognizable to our present selves. We shall have a partial world system of control, with interest focused on outer space; this present world will be to the galaxy much as Europe is to North America, the old world.

We shall have made vast technological advances and boredom will be rife. Social unrest will have reached an unprecedented height, among students and all other members of society. By comparison the troubles of 1969 and 1970 will seem as nothing.

The result will be world revolution if totalitarian control does not precede it. In any event, our only hope to avoid such an otherwise inevitable state is to increase our scientific knowledge in fields like psychiatry, more by then a branch of pharmacology, so that suitable diversions may be found, and perhaps new crosses to bear.

Our problem is to control our evolution, and this means to encourage freedom for the individual and provide an education for him to develop his power. Controls must be very limited. In most ways in the world today we have too many controls, and in the wrong places. To avoid boredom and atrophy in the light of cybernetic advances we need new crosses to bear, and this could be provided by the conquest of space, and perhaps the evolution of a new religion. Both of these factors could be held against the fears of either boredom and revolution or ultimate totalitarianism.

We are bound to build a new machine species, and the biggest single technical question we must face is how to control it. In finding a way we should have also found out how to make the most of human beings.

In constructive terms, we can easily say what it is we must do. We must always be aware of change and scientific development. We must always try to see the consequences of our policies, and here we see the need to develop education in breadth, depth, and for the sake of completeness, width as well. We must expect to be confronted, as the result of technological advance, with increased complexity and an ever narrower tight-rope to walk upon, hovering between boredom and enslavement. This requires research and discussion in the world of arts and religion and conducted in the background of an understanding of scientific method.

We may succeed with our immediate struggle to control both ourselves and our environment, and if we do we shall then be faced again in the twenty-first century with a new struggle for survival—a struggle against our own great strength and weakness, human curiosity and human imagination. A battle that can never end, except if it should be lost.

Further Reading

IT is not easy to provide further reading for a book of such wide scope and application. However, in trying to supply a few of the most important source books I should make it clear that I am not giving any of the literary references which have certainly played some part in influencing my point of view. Therefore before supplying a formal list of further reading references, for which purpose I have restricted myself to books and altogether eschewed reference to articles in the literature which would have made the further reading list absurdly large, I should make it clear that a whole set of novelists and poets have over the years influenced the views I have put forward in this book.

I should at least mention the novels of Anthony Powell, Iris Murdoch, Aldous Huxley, D. H. Lawrence, Francis King, L. P. Hartley, Graham Greene, Richard Aldington, Kingsley Amis and Christopher Isherwood, and be satisfied that I have given no more than a representative set of novelists whose work I have consistently read and who, with a very large number more, have influenced my views from the point of view of literature alone. W. H. Auden, Cecil Day Lewis, Louis MacNeice, as well as many of the so-called "classical" poets, of course, have also influenced my views as have many other writers of a philosophical, religious and scientific kind other than those who are included in the list of further reading. However, if asked to select those who have had the major influence, I have not hesitated to choose the following list, even though I do not suppose for a second that it is exhaustive.

ANSOFF, H.I., *Corporate Strategy*, Penguin Books, 1968.

BEER, S., *Decision and Control*, Wiley, 1966.

BLACK, M., *Language and Philosophy*, Cornell University Press, 1949.

BOOTH, A.D., *Digital Computers in Action*, Pergamon, 1965.

CRAWSHAY-WILLIAMS, R., *Methods and Criteria of Reasoning*, Routledge and Kegan Paul, 1957.

DANTZIG, T., *Number; the Language of Science*, George Allen & Unwin, 1930.

EDDINGTON, Sir Arthur, *The Philosophy of Physical Science*, Cambridge University Press, 1939.

FRAZER, Sir J.G., *The Fear of the Dead in Primitive Religion*, Macmillan, 1933.
GEORGE, F.H., *The Brain as a Computer*, Pergamon, 1961.
——, *Cybernetics and Biology*, Oliver & Boyd, 1966.
——, *Models of Thinking*, George Allen & Unwin, 1970.
HUXLEY, A., *Ends and Means*, Chatto & Windus, 1940.
HUXLEY, J.S., *Evolution; the Modern Synthesis*, Macmillan, 1942.
KORZYBSKI, A., *Science and Sanity*, The Science Press, 1933.
MADARIAGA, S. de, *Victors, Beware*, Jonathan Cape, 1946.
MORRIS, C.W., *Signs, Language and Behavior*, Prentice-Hall, 1938.
MUMFORD, L., *The Culture of Cities*, Secker & Warburg, 1938.
OGDEN, C.K. & RICHARDS, I.A., *The Meaning of Meaning*, Harcourt Brace, 1938.
OLIVER, W.D., *Theory of Order*, The Antioch Press, 1951.
PRICE, H.H., *Thinking and Experience*, Hutchinson, 1953.
RUSSELL, B., *Human Knowledge; its Scope and Limits*, George Allen & Unwin, 1948.
——, *The Autobiography of Bertrand Russell*, George Allen & Unwin, 1967.
——, *A History of Western Philosophy*, George Allen & Unwin, 1946.
RYLE, G., *The Concept of Mind*, Hutchinson, 1949.
SHERRINGTON, Sir Charles, *Man on his Nature*, Cambridge University Press, 1946.
TEILHARD DE CHARDIN, P., *The Phenomenon of Man*, Collins, 1959.
——, *The Future of Man*, Collins, 1964.
THORPE, W.H., *Learning and Instinct in Animals*, Methuen, 1956.
WIENER, N., *Cybernetics*, Wiley, 1949.
WITTGENSTEIN, L., *Philosophical Investigations*, Blackwell, 1953.